CRAWLERS

A CONCLUSIVE CASEBOOK

NATHANIEL BRISLIN

HANGAR 1 PUBLISHING

CONTENTS

Special thanks to Jaky and Nick Correll.
Without their sighting and support, this would have
never evolved into what it is now.

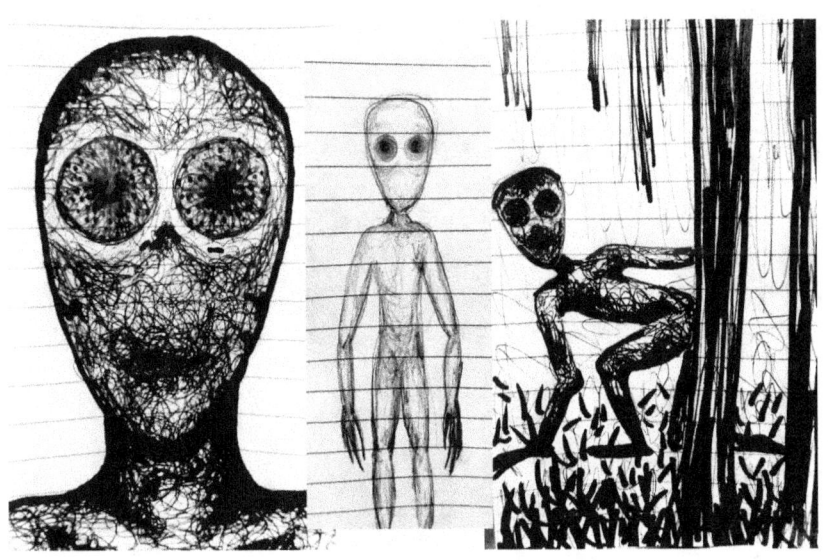

OF STONES UNTURNED

I understand that there are people who are skeptical of the fields of cryptozoology, the paranormal, and Fortean phenomena. I am able to very easily put my personal bias aside in order to objectively analyze evidence to discover what the truth is, whether it proves or disproves a claim.

It is everyone's right to have a skeptical mindset which should be encouraged especially with phenomena such as these.

I am attempting to gather true evidence to either prove or disprove and to have you make up your own mind based on that presented evidence.

I never claim to definitively know the answers to things like this. As an investigator of these "anomalous phenomena," I collect evidence, analyze data, match up similarities to make correlations, note inconsistencies and address them, and present my findings. As a researcher and writer, I objectively study these phenomena without an agenda to push. I do not know nor do I pretend to know the answers to these questions. As a researcher, it is my duty to present the evidence I find and the correlations that I see and allow the reader to decide for themselves based on the objective evidence given.

The Dover Demon is a case within the field of cryptozoology that has been remembered for its bizarreness as much as its brevity. Thankfully Loren Coleman, known as the modern master of cryptozoology, was involved firsthand in investigating and interviewing the eyewitnesses, having written extensively about the encounters and even coined the term "Dover Demon" itself.

On the night of April 21, 1977, at around 10:30 p.m., 17-year-old William Bartlett was driving himself and two peers down Farm Street in Dover, Massachusetts. Upon the top of the broken stone wall they were driving alongside, Bartlett saw a strange being crawling across. An hour later, the same or similar creature was sighted by 15-year-old John Baxter and 13-year-old Pete Mitchell on their walk home. Nearly 24 hours later 15-year-old Abby Brabham and her boyfriend were driving home when she encountered the creature on Springdale Avenue.

To this day the Dover Demon case persists as one of the most credible yet unexplainable cases in cryptozoology, remembered as being a brief blip on the Fortean radar, but what if that wasn't the end of the encounters with such a creature? Since then, throughout wildwoods of North America, there have been other sightings of pale humanoid creatures with large ovoid heads, reflective, illuminating eyes, and gaunt bodies with spindly limbs with bizarre movements and behaviors.

An interpretation of the Bartlett encounter as illustrated by artist and investigator Vincent Richardson.

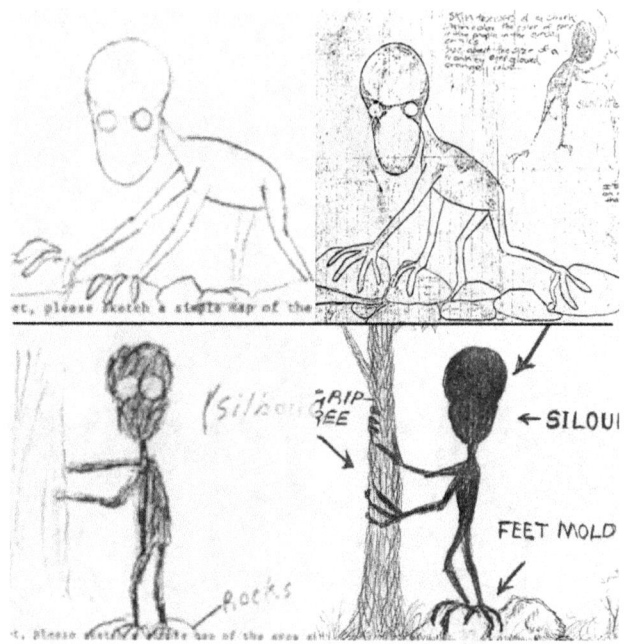

The original sketches done by the eyewitnesses of the Dover Demon. (Above: Sketches by John Baxter and Bill Bartlett. Below: Sketch by Abby Brabham)

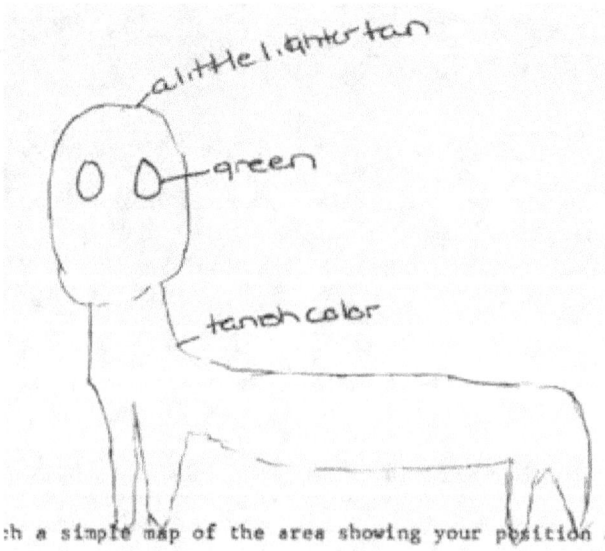

Not to be confused with the less credible and far less sighted Fresno Nightcrawlers, Pale Crawlers are gaunt, humanoid cryptids that have been sporadically sighted across the United States and Canada, generally within forested environments. Eyewitnesses typically report seeing a creature 3 - 6 ft. in height, either standing upright or moving on all fours with ease, with round heads, and pale or flesh-colored skin.

Crawler Height Comparison

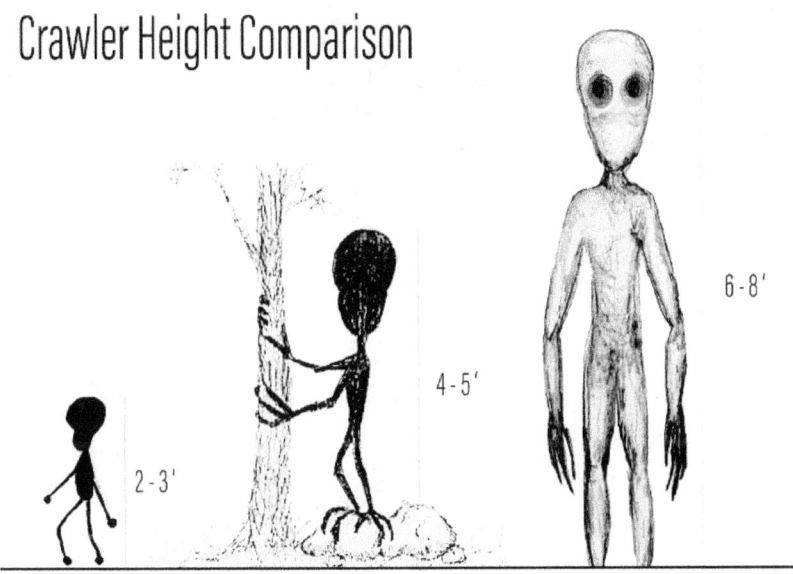

2-3'

4-5'

6-8'

"Pale Crawler," or simply a "Crawler," is a relatively new nomenclature that has been assigned to this phenomenon by investigators, cryptozoologists, and even witnesses themselves at least as early as 2018. The first usage of the name in this context is relatively difficult to pin down though the term has gained significant popularity since 2020.

While it's evident that Crawlers appear similar in description to Grey aliens, the resemblance is only superficial. Most of the more credible encounters lack to mention anything supernatural such as lights or UFOs so there's nothing to compare them to anything extraterrestrial quite yet. In fact, they're mostly described as entirely white or even a pinkish peach color as seen in the Dover Demon and a small handful of others.

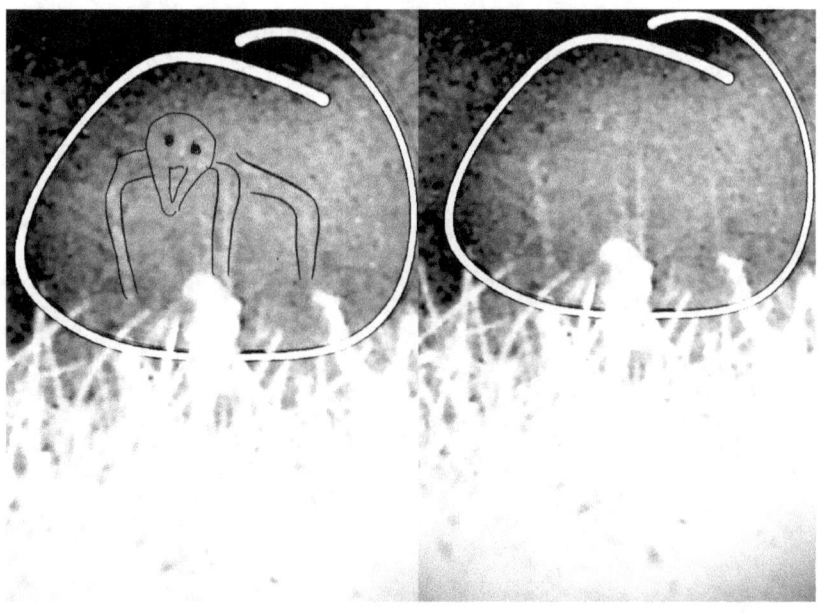

A possible Crawler captured on a game camera by a couple in rural Texas in June of 2018.

THE CRAWLER DISTINCTION

The world of cryptozoology is both a fantastic and ultimately a very curious place. All too often enthusiasts and researchers (such as Nate Brislin and myself) find ourselves at the mercy of what I often refer to as a "branch off"— that is, one cryptid is often labeled as another. Such is the case with these mysterious beings we so affectionately call Pale Crawlers. With their distinctly humanoid form, pale skin, and sometimes less than civilized behavior, these beings are many times referred to as Skinwalkers (Yee Naaldlooshii) and even Wendigo. Though it's easy to see where the mistakes are being made, neither of these things has much to do with these pale humanoids. Firstly, the Yee Naaldlooshii are more than mere primordial humanoids running about in the forests of this country. To the Navajo they were much more; they were entities to be feared. The mere mention of the name causes panic and widespread hysteria. These shamans or practitioners of what is known as "The Witchery way" bear little to no resemblance.

On the other end of this spectrum, we have the Wendigo or, as it is sometimes called, the Wettiko; a malevolent spirit that looms in the darkened corners of the great woods of the north watching and waiting for a human to dare to break the strict cultural taboos of their tribes' spiritual beliefs. Seen as a curse or even a possession, all semblance of humanity is stripped from the poor soul who finds himself at the mercy of a Wendigo possession. While the original depictions of the Wendigo do indeed describe them as pale, skinnier beings, the similarities between the Wendigo and Crawlers end there. After all, I've not heard any stories in which these pale beings are known to stalk their prey at every turn or taunt them with the terror that they and their families are next on the dinner menu.

With so much hard work and research at our disposal, I am both honored and privileged to write this for Nate. I've had the privilege of watching and sometimes assisting as Nate worked hard and persevered to bring you this book. I'm sure as you, the reader, delve into the information given to you here, you'll run into little snippets of bites that contain information about both the Yee Naaldlooshii and Wendigo. So with that, tie that rope around your waist, get your thinking caps on, and prepare to deep dive into the history and encounters with these pale, humanoid creatures. It's a deep and illustrious rabbit hole.

I'll see you on the other side.

Ryan Tremblay
Host of **Monster Radio**

1

"TIM" (ALIAS)

NAME OF EYEWITNESS	"Tim" (alias)
DATE/TIME OF SIGHTING	Fall, 1979. Nighttime.
LOCATION OF SIGHTING	Clearville, PA.
CIRCUMSTANCES PRIOR TO SIGHTING	Playing outside during a church function.
NOTABLE SIGHTING DETAILS	Green eyeshine and long legs.

Initial statement

"First of all I only added this awful drawing because it shows how the legs appeared. It's hard to draw a picture well when some details are lacking. Specifics on hands, mouth, and nose. I'm actually an artist. With paint. You'd never know it from this though. Anyway, the picture is only so you can see a better illustration of how it sort of looked.

It was a cool fall night in 1979 and my husband went with his parents to a church function. The kids all played outside while the parents did whatever it was they were doing in the social hall. My husband---I'll call him Tim for this account--had stayed outside after the other kids he was with went in to get a drink. Directly next to the church is the church cemetery. It's not huge, but some of the graves are very old. Within the cemetery, there are quite a few tall, full spruce trees that have probably been there for many, many years.

Tim heard some loud crashing noises from one of the trees nearby. He looked up in the tree and saw a set of eyeshine. It was almost like when a car pulls in a lot and the headlights shine. They were shining green, and in hindsight, he compares it to when the Predator was up in the tree. As he saw it, it jumped out of the tree and hit the ground, and paused. It looked back at him for a split second. It was a full, bright moon, and once it got out of the tree he could see it better on the ground. When it took off, he'd never seen anything like it. It went about 300 yards in several seconds in a curved pattern. The field is probably a half-mile long. After about 300 yards he lost sight of it.

It was about 7 ft. tall. The body was extremely skinny. Everything on it was skinny except for its head which resembled the head of ET. Large eyes that shone green. The strangest part was the backward bent legs. It's something you can't forget or mistake. They were bent back at a severe angle to the body, then sharply came back to the front. It had long feet. In the moment that it made eye contact with Tim, it paralyzed him with fear. He was so scared that he ran inside and told his dad--crying the entire time. His dad just laughed at him and surely thought he was just making it up.

The area this happened in is very rural and spooky. There is a big cave system behind the church that the boys would try to explore as kids. This was at Seven Dolors Catholic Church in Clearville, PA. Tim is a skeptic of anything paranormal or unexplained. He has to have proof to believe in things. He swears on his life that he saw this creature. It absolutely wasn't some kind of animal or bird. To this day when we go out to the church cemetery I glance up at the trees and wonder what exactly he saw that night many years ago. We think it must've been some kind of alien. There really is no other explanation. It was something not of this world."

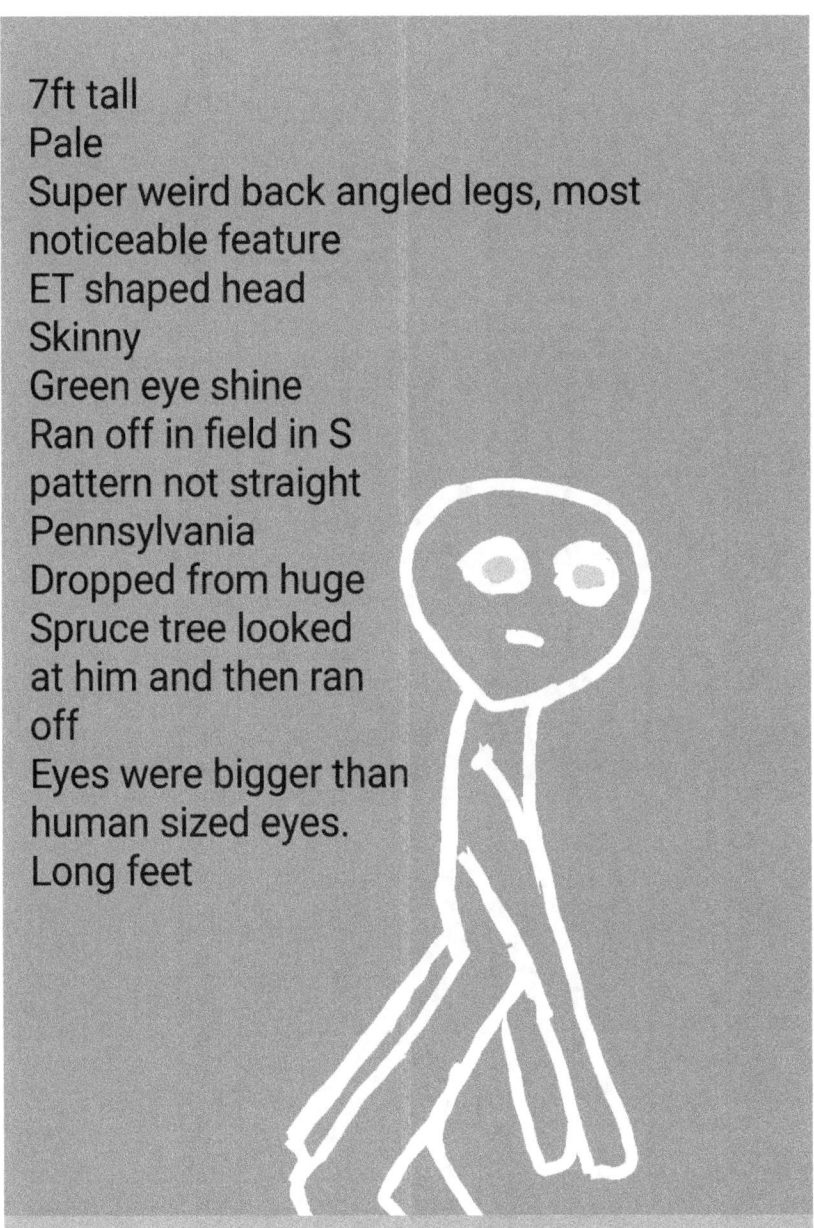

7ft tall
Pale
Super weird back angled legs, most noticeable feature
ET shaped head
Skinny
Green eye shine
Ran off in field in S pattern not straight
Pennsylvania
Dropped from huge Spruce tree looked at him and then ran off
Eyes were bigger than human sized eyes.
Long feet

Original sketch based on the eyewitness's description.

Updated sketch based on the eyewitness's description.

2

KIMBERLY ASHLEY

NAME OF EYEWITNESS	Kimberly Ashley
DATE/TIME OF SIGHTING	Around June 2001 at approx. 2:00 a.m.
LOCATION OF SIGHTING	Ballard County, Western Kentucky.
CIRCUMSTANCES PRIOR TO SIGHTING	Driving at night.
NOTABLE SIGHTING DETAILS	Recorded speed of approx 40 mph.

Initial statement

"My friend and I were driving around the back roads of Ballard County in Western KY. It was about 2 a.m. I was driving and turned onto a gravel farm road. As I did I caught sight of something white and vaguely human crawling in the ditch. As we passed I hit the brakes thinking it was a person who needed help. "Are you crazy?! Don't f--king stop!" Blake* screamed. (*Name changed for privacy)

I looked in the mirror and saw that it was standing up. Even though it was still in the ditch it was as tall as the stop sign next to it. It took a step towards us and I hit the gas. As we drove away I saw in the mirror that it dropped to all fours and was crawling after us. I didn't start pulling away from it til I got up to about 40 mph. No matter how close I was to it I never got a good look at it. It was fuzzy like it was constantly out of focus. I'm not sure why but something about it makes me think of it as male. Maybe the height? When it crawled it moved like a lizard-hands and feet flat on the ground, elbows and knees up and out, body wiggling side to side.

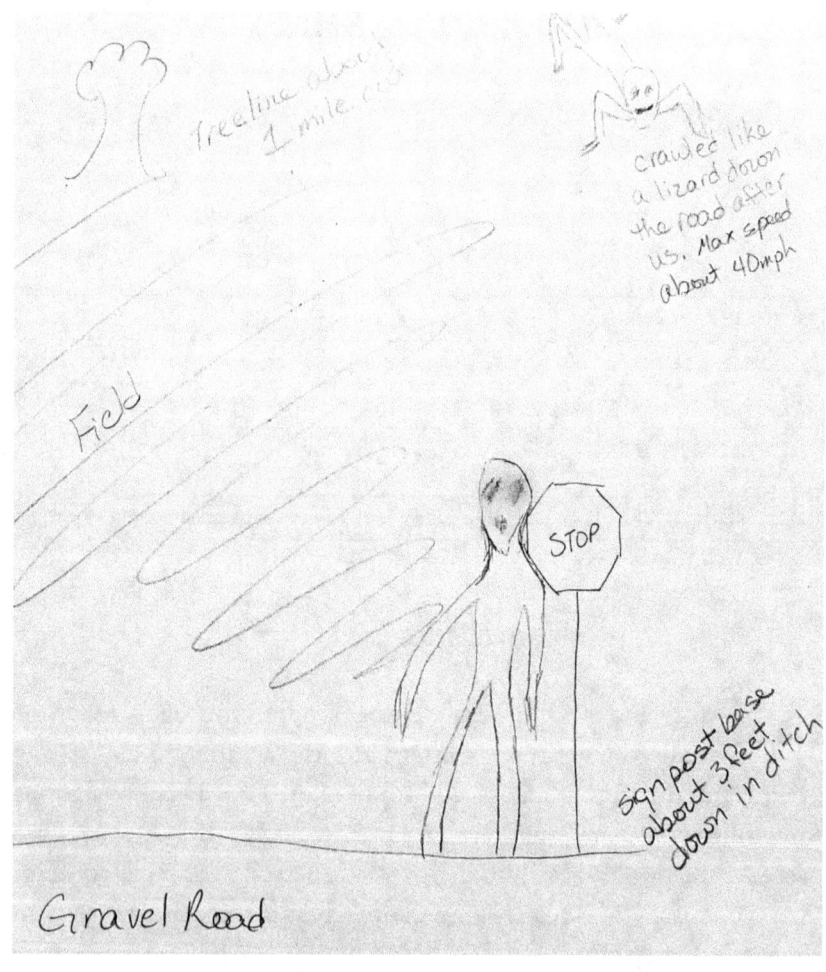

Sketch provided by the eyewitness.

This happened when I was around 22. I'm 40 now and have never seen that thing again. I've taken many a midnight cruise along those narrow roads but I've never had the nerve to go near that particular farm road again. Call me a chicken... I'll cluck happily.

Follow up dialogue

NB: Would you be able to describe what you saw in more detail?

KA: Its mouth wasn't that obvious until I saw it in the road... then it seemed to be grinning or maybe panting? The eyes were never more than a blur, it was determined to have a chat though... It chased us for a quarter mile and kept up until I passed 40 mph. At first, I wasn't sure what I'd seen and hit the brakes. I thought my friend was gonna have a coronary yelling at me to keep going... Of course, it was on his side so I don't blame him.

NB: How close do you think it got?

KA: From the passenger rear tire maybe 3 - 4 ft. It was RIGHT THERE behind the sign when I made the turn and it was a one-lane gravel farm road. My friend could have reached out and slapped the sign. I pulled away from it and lost sight in the rearview. The thing that really sticks out to me is the way it moved: like a lizard. It was standing on two legs in the ditch when we came up on it but when it started chasing it dropped to all fours. It was really skinny. It had spindly arms and legs and its hands and feet were turned out with elbows and knees up in the air. The hands and feet were about twice the length of a normal person's but that's just an impression. I don't remember details about them other than their size.

NB: Do you recall any skin texture or anything?

KA: It seemed smooth... Very reflective. It glowed white in the headlights and red in the tail lights.

NB: Its eyes and mouth didn't shine or reflect?

KA: No animal eyeshine from the eyes. They were significantly darker than the surrounding tissue. The edges weren't crisp; like it was just a little bit out of focus no matter how close. I don't think it made any noise. My friend never mentioned it and he's the one who would have heard it. I could hear it dislodging gravel as it came out of the ditch, so it had some weight even with being so skinny. I've seen and heard a lot of weird sh-t in the bottoms around home but that's the closest sighting I've ever had. Everything else was either just sounds or moving so fast that I never got a good look.

NB: Do you have any theories about what you saw in terms of what it could be?

KA: There's always been talk about weird "animals" all around the state. Of course, I'm more familiar with things in western KY where I grew up. My granddaddy told me about what's referred to in my family as the "Chalk Hill Booger." His grandfather was walking a mule back to the barn pulling a wagon loaded with tobacco. It was after dark and he didn't have any light, just going up the road by moonlight. Something black dropped out of the trees onto his mule and started eating it. He ran and when he got back with a light and a gun the mule was dead and half eaten laying in the road in front of the wagon still in the harness. I was always told that there used to be big black cats around there but I have no idea if that's true.

For a long time, my dad wouldn't walk down to the bottoms without a rifle. He went one morning before dawn to get in a deer stand while it was foggy. He said he was stalked by a pack of large "somethings" like big coyotes. He said they kept running at him out of the fog one after the other and did that until the fog lifted after sunrise. He stayed around the base of the stand after he got up in it. I don't know if you have any experience with coyotes but they generally won't come near people, not unless they're starving or rabid. He didn't have to shoot at them as they never got within striking distance but the gun goes with him if he's out in the dark and dad's no chicken. If he gets the gun then you know it's serious.

3

JULIE S.

NAME OF EYEWITNESS	Julie S.
DATE/TIME OF SIGHTING	Oct. 20, 2011, around 7-8 p.m.
LOCATION OF SIGHTING	"Catholic University" outside of Philadelphia, Pennsylvania.
CIRCUMSTANCES PRIOR TO SIGHTING	Driving.
NOTABLE SIGHTING DETAILS	Legs pulled against chest.

Initial statement

"I went to a University in Pennsylvania outside of Philadelphia. I will leave it up to you what one you think it is. It was a Catholic university so I never expected to see anything odd there ever of the paranormal sort.

This university had woods near it and a good amount to boot and two cemeteries near it, one being close to campus and one across the parking lot from the cafeteria. The one close to campus is important to the story as a nearby landmark. The second would be the road nearby that leads to a gate. This road is important to the second sighting.

The first time I saw this was on Legion Road. There is a small fenced-in area with a small building. I saw something gray at first that looked like a rock or stump. Even though I was in the car, I could see it looked like something sitting on the ground with its back to me. If you had Gollum from 'Lord of the Rings' sit on the ground with his legs pulled against his chest this is what it looked like to me.

The second event happened at night while on a ghost hunt the school had. We went outside and I remember it being windy and cold. We left from the back entrance to the main building and walked to a spot near a landscaped area with a trellis. We talked about where to go and started walking. The one cemetery mentioned before as a landmark is to the left of this spot across a road. I remember us going right from where we stood toward the road that led to the gate. It was in front of us. I saw this gray humanoid-looking creature run parallel to us and go down near the road before I lost sight of it. It was night so I know it was gray but what shade honestly I am not sure I would say slate gray. Size would be about 4 ft. tall, perhaps it was hunched a little while walking so this is an estimate. I looked far and wide for anything similar to this after the event happened and found nothing."

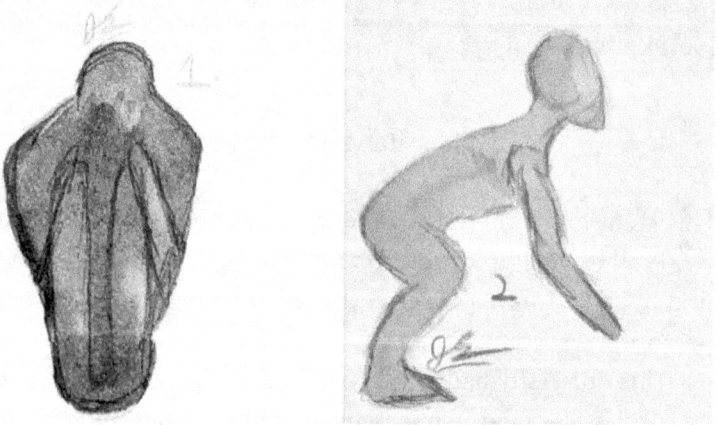

Eyewitness sketches provided by Ms. S.

Follow up dialogue

JS: First sighting happened about 8 a.m. timeframe at least the morning before noontime. Sunny with good visibility. 2nd sighting [was between] 6 - 8 p.m. dark night with high wind. I wasn't blind in the dark at the time and you could make out general shapes of things. This creature was lighter gray compared to the first one. That made it a little easier to see.

4

ANONYMOUS 1

NAME OF EYEWITNESS	Anonymous.
DATE/TIME OF SIGHTING	Spring, 2012 at approx. 9:30 p.m.
LOCATION OF SIGHTING	Along 520 Wiscasset Rd, Pittston, ME.
CIRCUMSTANCES PRIOR TO SIGHTING	Driving home from work.
NOTABLE SIGHTING DETAILS	Hairless "glistening/shiny" skin.

Initial statement

"When I was a senior in high school I used to work at a grocery store in Randolph, Maine and lived in Pittston which is a very rural area. I worked until close. It was about 9:30 and dark out when I was driving home. I was coming around a corner where the road drops down on either side into a gully and there are guard rails. As I was coming, my headlights caught something gray and gaunt crouched back to me on the right side by the guardrail. The skin was shiny and there was no hair. As soon as my headlights hit it, it looked over its shoulder and the eyes were yellow in the lights. It quickly reached up with both hands, grabbed the rail, and hopped over and down into the gully. I didn't even register what I saw right away but as I was driving I realized that it didn't resemble any animal I had seen before and it was squatting on two feet. Very weird. It had no clothing on and was almost white and glistening."

A Google Earth street view of where the encounter took place.

MICHAEL WALKER

NAME OF EYEWITNESS	Michael Walker
DATE/TIME OF SIGHTING	Several encounters occurred between mid-June and late August of 2014.
LOCATION OF SIGHTING	Vicksburg, Mississippi.
CIRCUMSTANCES PRIOR TO SIGHTING	Varied.
NOTABLE SIGHTING DETAILS	Multiple encounters within nearby areas. Posted to an internet forum.

<u>Initial statement</u>

"I think there's something strange living in the woods near my house. I live in a rural area in Mississippi and the area is surrounded by a vast forest that is littered with deer camps and thick foliage. I've seen something weird in there since I was 13 but before I get into that, I want to give some context. My family has lived on the property since my grandparents moved there to start a family. My dad and his siblings all grew up there, then my dad and mom moved into the house next door and my uncle moved into the house down the street. From there, I lived in the house for the next 18 years before I left for college and I've since moved to a nearby town. The property holds several acres of dense woodland, hills and steep embankments with several footpaths tracing throughout that lead to deer camps and hunting stands. Some of the paths also lead to hunting camps that belong to other people who live in the area.

When I was 13, I was walking along one of these footpaths when I heard a tree branch break and something landed with a loud THUD a couple yards off the path. I looked over just in time to see something humanoid barreling off into the forest on all fours. It was naked and its skin was paper white. That was all I could discern; I could only see it for a couple seconds before it disappeared. I didn't see it again for several weeks until I was coming out of the forest through a path behind my grandparent's house. It was raining and I was running to make it back home when I heard something shuffling around in one of the sheds in my grandparents' backyard. I thought this was weird considering the sheds were full of clutter and old junk that we didn't even use so there shouldn't have been anyone in there. I looked inside and that's when I saw what I've come to call the Pale Man up close. It was completely hairless and crouched down in the piles of junk with its back turned to me. It was very thin with a human-like body with visible ribs and strangely long limbs. It looked back over its shoulder to look at me and I could see that it had deep, black eye sockets with wide eyes staring back at me. It didn't have any lips, just teeth, and a mouth pulled back in a horrible grimace. It also didn't have a nose. It screeched at me and that's when I ran back to my house.

The next sighting isn't mine but one I learned of by complete happenstance. I was participating in a summer work program this past summer and I struck up a conversation with one of the other participants while we were waiting for orientation to begin. It came up that we were both interested in Native American folklore and urban legends when he asked me if I'd ever heard of the Rake. Since the Rake is the closest thing I've been able to find appearance-wise in regards to what I saw all those years ago, I told him my story. He looked shocked when I told him this and lamented that he had had a similar experience and the details shook me to my core.

It happened in 2014, the same year as my experience. It was deer season and he was sitting up in his deer stand before the sun had come up. While he was waiting, he heard something scaling the side of his deer stand which stood 15 feet in the air. He looked over and saw a skeletal face peering into the window; something was clinging to the side of his stand. Whatever it was, it was startled and fell to the ground. He heard it thump against the ground and watched it limp off into the forest. He described it as looking like the Wendigo from the video game Until Dawn (a point I also made to my college friend who introduced me to the game). I asked him if he could take me to the place he saw it but he said he doesn't visit that stand anymore because he's too afraid. I still asked him what general area it was in so I could drive through the area and see if I found anything and he did give me an answer and this is what really startled me. I can't give the exact address (again, for privacy reasons) but he said, "So, you know where ███████ Road meets ██████████ Road? It was right up the road from there." My house was DIRECTLY on the intersection of those two roads, meaning that whatever HE saw was in the general vicinity of the thing that I saw. I didn't get any more information out of him but I suspect that it happened at one of those deer camps that are connected to my property. This spurred me to look into the matter a bit more seriously.

I consider myself an amateur paranormal investigator and have been going on searches through the area in previous weeks. Every now and then, I'll hear something really big walking out of sight in the forest nearby, either obscured by trees or on the opposite side of a hill that I'm walking around, somehow always being out of sight. It will walk in sync with me and when I stop walking I'll hear it take a few steps before it stops, restarting only when I started walking again.

An incident like this happened about a week ago when I heard it trailing directly behind me as I made my way following a small creek just off one of the paths. There was a steep hill on my right side and I walked around the hill and started going in the opposite direction. I could still hear the creature on the other side of the hill. I looked up and I thought I saw something humanoid moving at the top of the hill, ducking to hide behind a thick tree. The hill was too steep for me to climb up to the top and investigate so I missed out on that opportunity. I'm not 100% sure that I ACTUALLY saw something in this instance. It was just a fleeting glimpse but I do know that I didn't hear any more footsteps following me after this.

I went for a full-blown stakeout yesterday. I camped in a clearing near a deer stand which is only a couple hundred yards from where my friend had his sighting and an even shorter distance from where I had my first sighting. I revisited the area where I had my sighting and saw something that piqued my curiosity. The area is full of very steep hills and washouts where rainwater erodes the dirt between these hills, making the area very precarious. There was a downward slope just off the path where I had my encounter and I saw a collection of sticks stacked together against a tree in the washout. I actually climbed down into the washout to investigate this further.

The sticks were assembled almost like a lean-to against the tree, but they also curved, kind of in a bowl shape. It looked like something had woven together a nest out of twigs. Something about the size of a man could fit into. It also used larger branches, sometimes three inches thick, to strengthen the structure. I don't know of any local animal that could have built something like this and I don't think it was naturally occurring. If this was the work of the Pale Man, I don't think he'd used it recently. I couldn't find any bones, droppings, footprints, or any sign of something actually living in it. I did take pictures of this nest though and can upload them.

I then returned to my tent and watched the area until the sun went down and I went to sleep, planning to wake up around 3 a.m. to perform my stakeout. When the time came, I stayed inside my tent and looked out into the night through my tent window. I soon discovered that it was incredibly hard to see in this much darkness and I couldn't see anything clearly far beyond my tent. I did see something, however: an indiscernible shape situated at the base of two conjoined trees. It was way too far away for me to discern what exactly it was, but I know it was about 2 - 3 ft. tall.

I'm sure you're wondering why I didn't use a flashlight to which my answer is the only one I had available was the one on my cell-phone. It wouldn't have been strong enough to reach whatever was resting at the base of the tree and if the creature was watching me from nearby a flashlight certainly would have alerted it and I was afraid of distressing it and possibly causing it to attack (although admittedly, in the times it has been following me through the woods, it's never seemed keen on actually attacking me. It just seems to be curiously observing just out of sight.) I kept my eyes locked on this shape for several minutes and it didn't move an inch. After about a half an hour of nothing happening, I determined it must have been a bush that looked weird in the complete darkness. I was tired and what animal could have possibly kept that still for so long? Soon after that, I fell asleep and then I woke up at 8 the next morning. While I was packing up my things, I looked at the two trees where the thing rested beside. There was absolutely nothing there; not a bush, not a tree stump. The spot where I saw SOMETHING was completely barren. Maybe there actually was something watching me. I don't know. I don't know if it means anything. I don't know if anything happened or if it was a trick of the eyes or what have you. This is just what I noticed.

That's my story. Like I said, I consider myself an amateur paranormal investigator. I'm only posting this on here because I'd like the community's input on where I should go next with this investigation, as well as any information that you think would help. Whatever I saw very closely resembles the Rake, in fact, that's really the only thing I've been able to find that matches up with it. That being said, it's very difficult to find any reliable information on the matter so I figured I would come here. I will be continuing my searches through the area and I will be continuing stakeouts and I do expect to keep you guys updated if anything comes up. Please, feel free to post any questions, theories, hunting tips, [or] anything that you think will help. I want to know what this thing is."

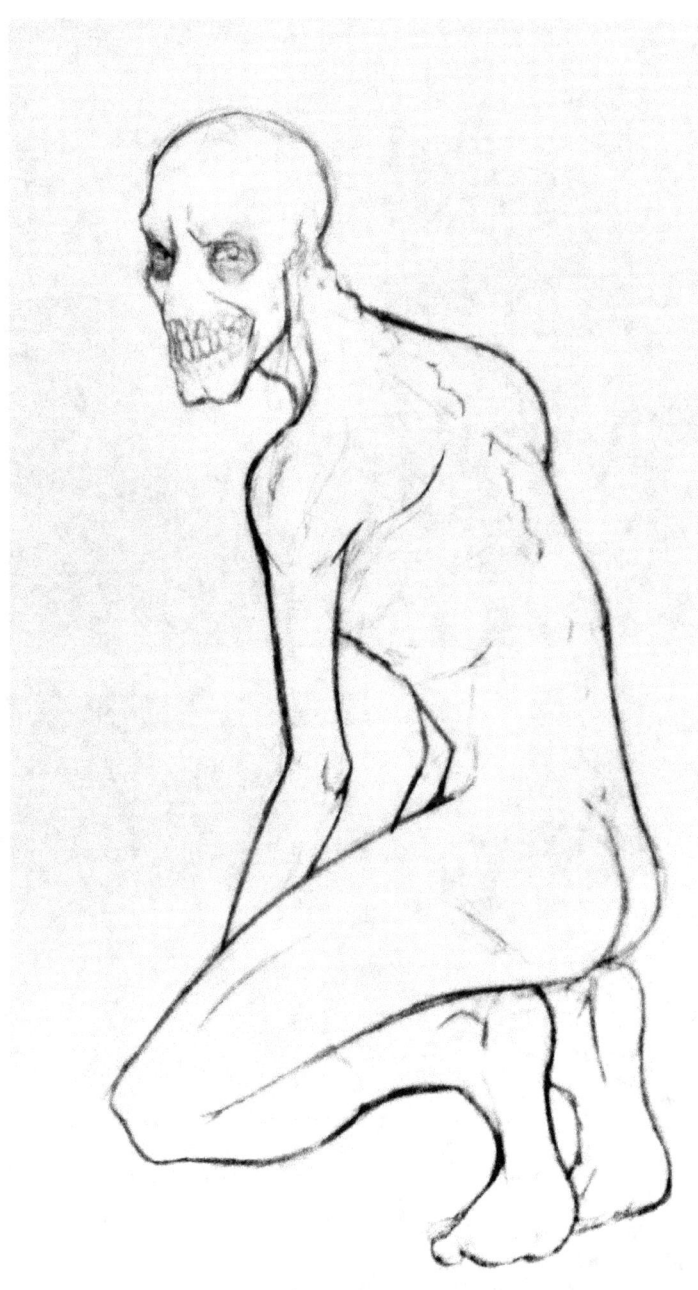

Eyewitness sketch provided by Mr. Walker.

Alleged nesting structures discovered by Mr. Walker.

Photo taken by Mr. Walker of where he saw the creature. The line is an indicator of how tall it was.

"UPDATE: The first two are of the nest (that collection of sticks on the left side of the first picture, that is leaning against the tree), one from the side and one from the back. It's situated like a lean-to with some sticks situated to the sides and on the floor. This rests right beside a runoff which would be a source of running water when it rains so I don't expect that it's a permanent shelter if a shelter at all. I inspected the nest and found that several twigs had been jumbled together and stacked to make the structure and that this wasn't naturally occurring. Again, I didn't find anything else to suggest that it had lived there recently. There were no fresh footprints, feces, or animal remains left behind (on that note, until other evidence presents itself, I'm assuming the creature is omnivorous and am looking for evidence that it eats either animals or vegetation alike, although I still haven't found anything.)

On the subject of theories, one of you has suggested that it could possibly be a hairless chimpanzee (Thank you for the nightmares that THAT google image search presented me with, by the way). But joking aside, I don't believe that this is the case. The thing I saw was a very different shade of white and wasn't as muscular as you find chimpanzees to be. It looked very thin and fragile. It didn't look particularly strong plus it was much taller in comparison. On top of all of that, I haven't seen anything resembling chimpanzee footprints in the area, which is another thing that I wanted to point out: I've never seen any footprints of this creature. I've only ever seen deer, hog, raccoon, and the occasional coyote footprint in those woods. That being said, I believe that there's possibly a reason for that as well. I think the creature might be chiefly arboreal. It has shown that it has a knack for climbing. The first time I saw it it had fallen from a tree, indicating to me that it had been traveling through the treetops to begin with, and my friend said that it climbed all the way up the side of his deer stand which would have been no easy feat, I imagine. Even if the creature did occasionally travel on the ground the distance between any given set of footprints it would leave behind would be very outstretched and would make tracking this thing extremely difficult. That being said, I would also like your opinions on this.

Also, quick side note: the last picture is of where I saw the "bush" from my camping trip. The red line is there to indicate about how tall whatever I saw was. I took this picture from inside my tent, where I was when I had the encounter and was only a couple yards away from it. It may be redundant, but I would still like to point out that there was absolutely nothing in that spot when I took this picture that I could have otherwise envisioned. There must have been something there."

Follow up dialogue

NB: I was wondering if you would be able to give me specific dates and times these events occurred.

MW: I'm afraid I can't give specific dates, since it's been so many years. But I'll do my best to tell you what I know. My initial sightings occurred in the summer of 2014. I'm guessing the first would have been mid-June, and the second happening mid or late July. I'm not sure what month my friend's sighting was but it was during deer season so that puts it anywhere from October - December. My stake-out, where I found the nest, happened during the period of August 21 - 22nd.

NB: Have you had any other encounters?

MW: This wasn't in the post but a friend and I also went camping in the area in late September, and we believe the creature stalked us for a couple of hours that night as well. I had gotten there a few hours before my friend Darrian and by the time I had set up the tent the sun had long since set. So I was waiting in the tent for my friend and an hour in I hear something stumbling down the trail. I thought it was my friend struggling to carry some of the stuff he brought with him so I called out to him. Whatever it was made its way to the front of the tent and stopped there. I said his name again and it shuffled over to the side of the tent and stopped. By now, I'm worried and I grab my walking stick in case I have to defend myself. I say, "Darrian, for real, if you try to scare me I'm gonna beat the s--t out of you" and just as I said that my phone rings. It's Darrian. I answer and he tells me that he's about to leave the house and he asks me if I need him to bring anything else. Whatever had been standing outside my tent immediately turns and starts running down the trail. Nothing happens until my friend gets to the camp. I help him unpack and we cook dinner and then we decide to take a late night stroll through the path where I found the nest (The path starts next to where we set up the tent and circles around so we could go the full length of it). As we're walking past the nest, we hear something walking around behind us, following us. Something big. Something walking on two legs. It only walks when we walk and it stops when we stop. We can hear it but we can't see it even when we shine our lights down the trail. Then it starts circling us. It doesn't care now, it's just steadily walking in big circles even when we're stopped in the middle of the path. There are steep, washed-out hills on either side of us but they don't seem to slow it down (whereas my friend and I, who went back there the next day, took ten or so minutes to climb back up those hills and that was WITH the help of a rope we had tied to a tree and used to scale them). This goes on for about three minutes and once whatever it was was behind us my friend and I ran down the trail as fast as we could. Whatever it was didn't follow us and we didn't have any more trouble with it the rest of the night.

NB: When did that occur?

MW: I can't remember the exact date but it was mid-late September.

6

ANONYMOUS 2

NAME OF EYEWITNESS	Anonymous.
DATE/TIME OF SIGHTING	Late summer/early fall, 2014. Nearly dusk.
LOCATION OF SIGHTING	North of Binghamton, New York.
CIRCUMSTANCES PRIOR TO SIGHTING	Out on a walk.
NOTABLE SIGHTING DETAILS	Sighted on two occasions.

Initial statement

"It was in the summer and early fall of 2014. I was walking down the road two of the times I saw it, driving the third, each time late evening. Not quite dusk but getting there. Same stretch along some swampy woods near my home, north of Binghamton, NY.

There is an old pasture that separates the road from the woods by about 50 - 70 yards or so. The two times I saw it while walking it kept pace with me from just within the trees for about a mile each time. I could tell it was there but couldn't get a good look at it. I've had coyotes and feral dogs do the same thing. I always assumed it was because they are trying to decide whether or not to attack, which is more than a little unnerving when it's an unknown humanoid thing. I would know how to react to a coyote or dog coming at me; I had no clue what would have happened if this thing came at me.

The time I saw it when driving it was out in the open when I spotted it but it went back into the trees very quickly. That was the best look I got of it but some brush obscured the hips and legs. It was short, maybe 5 - 5.5 ft. tall and I could tell it wasn't proportioned like a human. Its torso was too short and the arms were too long. I didn't get a great look at the head, it was facing away from me and either the head was low without much neck or it was just holding its head down as it ran. It was uniformly pale, off-white in color. At the distance and lighting conditions it was in I couldn't tell if it was fur, skin, or whatever but it appeared to be the same color all over.

I haven't seen it since, but I have occasionally had the 'red-alert' feeling when in the same woods hunting, even though there wasn't any visible reason. Not sure if there is a connection because I get a similar feeling when I run across coyotes or bears and the like but it always struck me as odd that I couldn't notice the cause (consciously, at least. Part of me definitely noticed something.)"

7

J.D.

NAME OF EYEWITNESS	J.D.
DATE/TIME OF SIGHTING	September 2013.
LOCATION OF SIGHTING	Peoria, Arizona.
CIRCUMSTANCES PRIOR TO SIGHTING	Getting ready for bed.
NOTABLE SIGHTING DETAILS	Subject was inside the eyewitness' room at the foot of their bed.

Initial statement

"It was a cool suburban Arizona night in 2013 and everything was going as normal. It was getting a bit late so I got ready for bed as I usually do. Afterward, I climbed into bed and fell asleep, like I always do.

In the middle of the night, I awaken to a disturbing presence of someone or something watching me. I look to the foot of my bed and see this crouching white thing with only a possible head visible. I sat in silence and fear for what seemed like hours, staring at it. Its face was a weird round shape, kind of like how people usually portray aliens' heads (I'm not saying it was an alien. I don't know what it was).

Its face was featureless with the possible outline of a nose and brow visible. After a long time of staring and hoping for it to go away, I eventually dozed off. When I woke up in the morning there was no sign of it or anything that could resemble it. I went to the foot of my bed and set pillows and blankets up to try and recreate and hopefully debunk it but to no avail.

Follow up dialogue

NB: How tall would you say it was?

JD: It appeared to be crouching behind the foot of my bed so I'm not exactly sure but its head was around a foot and a half tall.

NB: Do you know how tall the foot of your bed is?

JD: Around three feet tall.

Eyewitness sketch provided by J.D.

8

ANONYMOUS 3

NAME OF EYEWITNESS	Anonymous.
DATE/TIME OF SIGHTING	Late December 2015.
LOCATION OF SIGHTING	South of Swan Lake, Montana.
CIRCUMSTANCES PRIOR TO SIGHTING	Listening to music while driving down a logging road.
NOTABLE SIGHTING DETAILS	A Dover Demon-like creature.

Initial statement

"I was 18 when this story took place in the winter of 2015. It's not super long and not particularly scary, though I sure was terrified when it happened. It was on a logging road south of Swan Lake, Montana, sort of near Beaver Creek, I believe. There was a decent amount of snow on the ground. I was visiting home, Swan Lake, for a couple days, and my little sister (17) and I wanted to go for a drive and listen to music. So we drive for a good twenty minutes away and find this back road and pull off a good distance from the main road so no one would see us. It was pitch black out and in winter it's so dead silent at night it's eerie, especially out in the boonies like that. I left my headlights on because I had this creepy feeling like we were being watched but just figured it was a deer or something. I'd seen moose on that road before so I knew it was busy.

My sister and I were having a conversation when I looked out into the trees and I swear I see this emaciated pale white humanoid type thing just barely trying to hide behind a tree. It was still in the darkness beyond my headlights so it kind of melted into the shadows. I stared at it for a long time. My sister was involved with something she was talking about so she was oblivious to my change in mood. I couldn't take my eyes off of it. It had this misshaped head that was too big for its thin body and its eyes were two huge black unblinking marbles. It didn't move or do anything so I kind of told myself it was just something I was seeing in the shadows. It was just beyond the light enough that I could write it off that easily I guess.

I went back to talking with my sister for a while and decided to see if I could still see the shape of the creature in the shadows and the next time I looked up it was closer, now just at the edge of the light. I felt so scared that my eyes filled with tears. It was sort of hunched to its right side and was standing with a rounded back with its boney, weird hands in a claw shape. I had pulled into the beginning of a single-lane road that was plowed ten feet in. There was no room for me to turn around so I had to back out. I made the terrible mistake of just gunning it backward. Every time I kept looking back it was closer and closer. I ripped the plastic covering off of the driver's side mirror almost hitting a tree in my rush. I hate to say that I left it there, I was too scared to stop and pick it up. Sorry, Mother Nature.

My sister never saw the thing. She was super confused about why I randomly decided to get quiet and then book it out. We drove for a while longer but I didn't pull off anywhere, I still felt really creeped out. It took me a while to get comfortable going out in the woods alone or driving down backroads alone at night again. I definitely still have no clue what it was. It wasn't some confused hiker wandering around naked but it had the upright body of a person. Looked kind of like those Dover Demon sketches but I was between Swan Lake and Seeley Lake, Montana, and it was white and ashen."

Original sketch provided by the eyewitness.

9

ANONYMOUS 4

NAME OF EYEWITNESS	Anonymous.
DATE/TIME OF SIGHTING	February 14th, 2015 between 7:30 - 9 p.m.
LOCATION OF SIGHTING	Vancouver, British Columbia, Canada.
CIRCUMSTANCES PRIOR TO SIGHTING	Waking up from a nap.
NOTABLE SIGHTING DETAILS	Glowing white/yellow light emanating from the subject.

Initial statement

"I had a very disturbing encounter about six years ago, with a tall humanoid being 8 - 9 ft. tall in my home. It matches all the descriptions of a Crawler, almost anorexic with elongated arms and fingers but the encounter I had was strange. I remember waking from my nap to hearing what I assumed was my boyfriend returning with food. My house has my bedroom on the basement level and my kitchen, living room, entranceway/front door, and home bathroom are on the floor above me. There are cushioned stairs descending to my bedroom that when walked on make a loud tromping noise and my boyfriend has a familiar way of running down them that I always recognize.

I had taken a nap while he went to go get food when I was woken up by the loud tromping of what sounded exactly like his feet running down my stairs. Anyone with partners or kids/family members knows you can identify every person's distinct way of walking. So I get out of bed and walk to my bedroom entrance all groggy. I knock over one of the cans on my bedside table waking up (this is an important detail for later).

My bedroom entrance faces slightly away from where the stairs end, I have two glass doors. I go to open them when I see an 8 - 9 ft. tall being (I'm 5'10") staring over my head (not at me which I remember distinctly) and I was craning my neck to look at its face. It has glowing white/yellow light emanating off of it. I remember my hallway downstairs is illuminated. Its body is skinny and pale white/beige. It has no mouth and eyes I don't quite remember but are black and empty. It had outrageously long arms and fingers and I remember being scared it would touch me with them.

This is the strongest memory I have: its arms are in a hugging position like a parent or S.O. who wants you to come into their arms, wide and open. Most people would scream or run or do anything but just stare silently but this was all I felt I could do. I felt drugged almost. I crane my neck, staring at it for what feels like a short time before I start getting feelings of calmness and tranquility, even care/love flowing through my mind and body. I get the urge to go back to bed and sleep. I remember being mortified once I realized the thing in my bedroom doorway wasn't my boyfriend who had gone out to get food so I don't know why I'd just return back to bed so calmly. It is almost like it sensed my fear and with its outstretched arms calmed me down telepathically almost with a "stay calm and behave it's alright" message.

Despite the warmth of the encounter I still felt like I had to be respectful. This being was vastly more powerful than me, or at least that's what it felt like it conveyed. Once I was in bed and glanced back at my doorway I saw it had left/dematerial-ized. In hindsight, I remember feeling like a child obeying its parent during the encounter even though I was 19. When my boyfriend finally got back he woke me up and I was terrified. This time I yelled like all the repressed fear I had from earlier manifested? Importantly, that can I knocked over when I went to go to the bedroom entrance was still on the ground. I picked it up when my boyfriend got back.

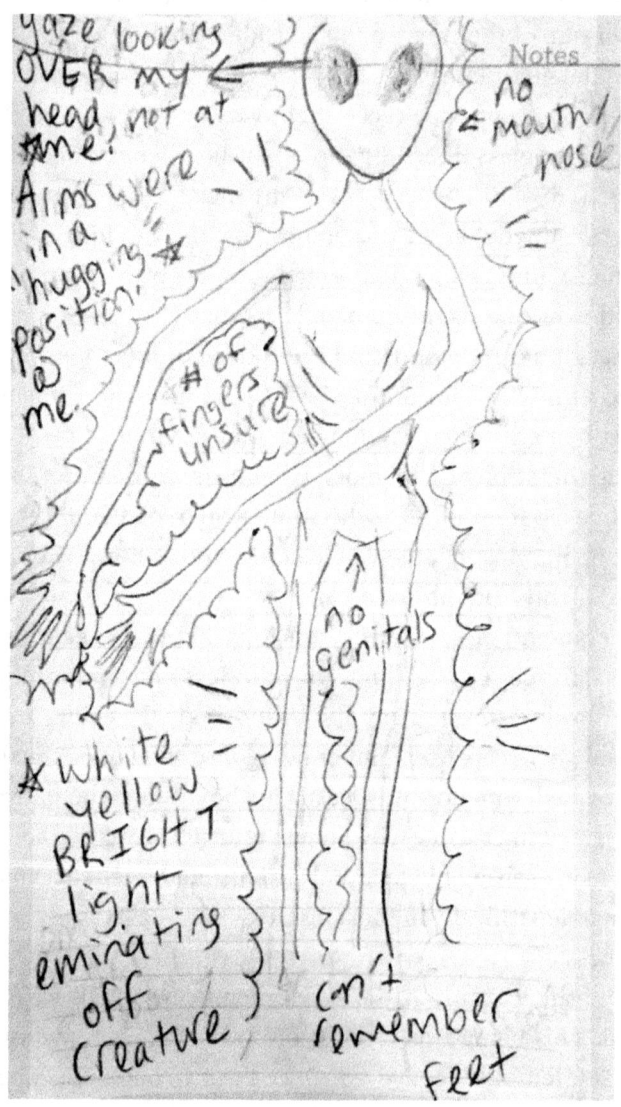

Original sketch provided by the eyewitness.

I'm interested in knowing if what I saw was a Crawler or if it could've been an angel of some kind. Alien was one of my thoughts but it was glowing, huge, and didn't have a terrifying menacing quality to it other than when I first realized it wasn't my boyfriend. As I mentioned, I felt warm and cared for strangely. Sleep paralysis is also possible, but wouldn't I then have been paralyzed and unable to move and unable to knock over the can?"

10

ANONYMOUS 5

NAME OF EYEWITNESS	Anonymous.
DATE/TIME OF SIGHTING	"July or August" of 2015 at approx. 1 a.m.
LOCATION OF SIGHTING	Westville, Nova Scotia, Canada.
CIRCUMSTANCES PRIOR TO SIGHTING	Staying over at an ex's house.
NOTABLE SIGHTING DETAILS	Glowing yellow orb seen.

Initial statement

"I spent the night at my ex's place in a very rural small town outside of New Glasgow, NS called Westville. We were up very late watching UFC (probably 1 a.m.) and I went into the back bedroom of the house on the second floor and happened to have glanced out the window towards the backyard.

His backyard was long and rectangular in shape and had an embankment that sloped down to a tree line at the end of the yard which was nothing but woods from beyond that point.

When looking out the window I noticed something very pale white crawling through the tree line. It immediately caught my eye and I kept staring at it. I called my ex at the time to come in and look. We both got really quiet and we came to realize that we weren't witnessing a creature that either of us could recognize. It was human-like in form, very skinny, purely pale and crouched forward with very long arms and would make a few movements forwards towards the yard and then back deeper into the woods again.

We had horrible phones back then at the time. I had an old Black-berry and his was no better and they both couldn't record what our eyes were seeing in the pitch black of night in the country. The only thing I could think of to do at this time was to call my older brother who has an interest in paranormal topics. I called him and described to him everything that we were seeing and to this day he doesn't disbelieve my accounts in any fashion. Something I said over and over to him on the phone was "it's not moving like a human, its move-ments are really really strange." They were almost spastic in nature, nothing natural or orderly that I could make sense of compared to how other mammals move. It made no noise that I could hear through the window.

Something else that was also really messed up about my experi-ence that I have zero explanation for is that the Crawler could be seen down on the left-hand side crawling around the treeline but for a few moments we saw a glowing deep yellow orb floating between the treeline for a few moments as well. I'm wondering if there are any other accounts like this.

As I've mentioned in my story, this was an ex so we are no longer together so I have no idea if he continued living there or ever saw such a sight again in his backyard. I've always been curious if it's still out there and I often think about my experience as I can recall it in high detail like it was yesterday. I'll never forget what I saw until the day I die."

11

ANONYMOUS 6

NAME OF EYEWITNESS	Anonymous.
DATE/TIME OF SIGHTING	Between August and October in mid-2015 or 2016 at approx. 11 p.m.
LOCATION OF SIGHTING	North of Monticello, Arkansas.
CIRCUMSTANCES PRIOR TO SIGHTING	Driving from father's house to mom's.
NOTABLE SIGHTING DETAILS	Eyewitnesses encountered something chasing their car.

Initial statement

"Okay, I want to preface this by saying I have had a lot of sh-t happen to me on my grandparents' land. It's 75 acres of horror if you're not used to it. I grew up so a lot of this didn't phase me too much. So if my reactions are odd it's because this is my life and I'm kind of desensitized. No, this is not the only thing to chase after me in my car but this one was different. Okay. Anyway, on with it.

I was 17 years old, driving from my dad's house on the aforementioned land. Pretty late, I think it was around 11 or so. I had dropped someone off at my dad's house and was driving back into town to get back to my mom's place.

As I was driving down our long driveway I kept seeing things move in the field. I didn't pay any attention, probably a rabbit or something. Things moving in the grass is normal.

I get out to the road and I see something/someone in the ditch just laying there. Me, being a girl in a raggedy old car at a place with piss poor signal in the middle of the night with no weapon on me, I floor it. I don't care, I figured I could call my dad later to take care of the possible drunk in the ditch.

I'm driving down the road, memory of the ditch person creeping me out, I get this awful feeling of being watched. I'm traveling down this road at nearly 60 mph with no signal whatsoever. Okay. Maybe I'm just overreacting, whatever. I still speed up because I want to get a signal to call my boyfriend because it would make me feel safer.

Then I see... something... running alongside my car. Well, I say running. It was more... skittering. Lanky limbs, on all fours running and keeping up with me going 60+ down a country logging highway.

I think my brain kind of had an aneurysm at this point, because I'm just repeating to myself "What the f--k, what the f--k," I'm getting closer to civilization though so I floor it, getting up to 80 and leaving it behind. I called my boyfriend, freaking out about what I saw. I pulled over at a little church with a light out front, trying to logic it out, when I see the thing again. It's on the road, skittering towards my parked car. Before I have time to pull out of the lot, it's on me, hitting my car hard enough to dent the rear bumper. I scream, squealing out of the lot and driving like a maniac toward town. I get into town and circle around the main areas a few times, calming down before I go to moms."

Follow up dialogue

"I think it happened mid-2015 or 16 because I was either 16 or 17 when it happened. Probably late summer or early fall between

August and October. I'd like to reiterate, a lot of stuff happened there and after so much happens the details get a little fuzzy."

Additional information

"Further description of the thing: it was weirdly flat, like someone trying to do a backbend but... not bending. Its limbs were long and spindly with pale skin stretched too tight across its bones."

12

JAKE SALYERS

NAME OF EYEWITNESS	Jake Salyers
DATE/TIME OF SIGHTING	October 2015 at approx. 9:00 p.m. Boyfriend had a childhood encounter.
LOCATION OF SIGHTING	Central Illinois.
CIRCUMSTANCES PRIOR TO SIGHTING	Driving back home at night.
NOTABLE SIGHTING DETAILS	Several other local sightings.

Initial statement

"So one night in October 2015, my boyfriend and I were driving back from Wisconsin to my family's house in central IL. It was around 9 p.m., pitch black, and freezing cold with rain. We were about 15 minutes away from our destination. We were on a road we drive on often. That road is completely rural with big stretches of forests and fields. No street lights or anything.

My boyfriend and I were in mid-conversation, rambling about god knows what, when we both stopped talking abruptly. We both saw it at the same time. Leaning out of the dark woods to our right was a naked, pale, emaciated humanoid. There was no recognizable face. I think it was so pale that the headlights reflected off of its head making the features hard to discern. It was hairless. We saw its head, shoulders, and boney, lanky hand. We drive by that spot often and we know there's nothing there that we could've mistaken. It's far from any houses. Any naked person would've gotten hypothermia in that cold. We sat in silence for a few seconds, instinctively pretending nothing happened. Then I said, "Did you see..." and my boyfriend responded, "Thank god you said something!" because he was about to be in denial about it. The thing is, that's not the end of the story. It turns out my boyfriend has seen something similar when he was a kid.

When he was younger, he lived in a town near that road on a rural property surrounded by woods. His dad was a hunter and had a fridge full of deer meat in the garage that had been neglected. His dad was procrastinating having to deal with it so for a while it sat festering. So one night he's in bed and he hears noises in the garage. Assuming it was his dad, he got up to check out what was going on. When he turned on the light and he saw something move so fast he could barely process it. He saw something white and hairless scramble across the garage. It then pulled itself under the half-open garage door. We're thinking it was trying to get to the rotting deer meat.

Then, shortly after we had our sighting on that road, two of our friends were hanging out at one of the parks outside of that same town where my boyfriend grew up. Pretty far from the center of town. They were parked, just talking, when they saw a lanky, white humanoid gallop across a distant field and into the woods. Then I made a Facebook post about it asking if anyone else had seen something similar. Turns out, one of my high school friends had seen one gallop out of a cornfield about 20 minutes away! Then I did some research. Turns out, someone in a nearby town reported a sighting online. Then I found another on the other side of the state. It was seen by a cemetery that has caves nearby.

I truly believe these things are real and I consider myself very lucky to have seen one. I have my theories about them, but I'll leave it up to you to hypothesize!

P.S. Recently (2019) my boyfriend and I camped out at his childhood home. We heard an unexplainable baby cry coming from the woods. There was something very off about it, like something trying to mimic a baby."

Eyewitness sketch provided by Mr. Salyers.

13

"SARAH NIELSEN" (ALIAS)

NAME OF EYEWITNESS	"Sarah Nielsen" (alias)
DATE/TIME OF SIGHTING	Tuesday, September 29th, 2015.
LOCATION OF SIGHTING	Uinta Wasatch Cache National Forest, Utah.
CIRCUMSTANCES PRIOR TO SIGHTING	Tracking wounded deer on a hunting trip.
NOTABLE SIGHTING DETAILS	Detailed leadup to a very brief sighting. Severe post-sighting emotional impact.

Initial statement

"Let me first clarify that this was four years ago (2015) when I was fifteen on a muzzleloaders mule deer hunt in the far northeastern part of Utah which contains some of the most remote and beautiful places in the state. I've been frequently out in this area spreading in Summit county that cuts in and out of lower Wyoming since before I can remember including lots of hiking, backpacking, camping, hunting and being involved in some of my grandfather's work. I am skeptical of things not proven by methods of science but I don't deny all of those things. I find that it's impossible for science to know of all that is out there in our vast world.

My grandfather is a recently retired biologist and former conservation officer for the state, [as well as] a regional specialist, and was over wildlife and habitat management for many years. He's done everything from habitat management programs (controlled fires to benefit areas) to quite literally wrangling moose to be transplanted and darting black bears. He has seen mountain lions, bears, birds of all kinds, small mammals, ruminants, plants, and natural phenomena for [the] majority of his life. He understands so much that many people, including myself, will never be able to even imagine. He's scientific, honest, straightforward, and level-headed. He's agnostic and is not superstitious and often used to (lovingly and respectfully) tease a certain C.O. who thinks certain Bigfoot, Skinwalkers, and other beings exist. Other than this experience, he has never encountered an animal that he could not at least partially (if not completely) identify, and other than the natural, innate fear of being in close quarters with a bear, drunken and belligerent hunter, or incredibly potent tranquilizer medication, he's told me over and over he's never been terrified of an animal or experience like this; only curious or surprised.

It was late September and we were in a small camp by a lake in the high Uinta mountains, hunting both grouse and mule deer with muzzleloaders. The camp was a small collection of men and women my grandfather had worked with over the years as a supervisor/biologist/C.O. and these were people I grew up with.

One of the women (a new wife to one of the guys) had shot a buck deer, injuring but not killing it immediately and they had lost track of it. Devastated by the thought of wasting the animal, she returned to camp in the afternoon upset and concerned that the deer had run into an even more secluded area of the mountain which was hard to reach from the trail that she had shot from, a place my grandfather was familiar with because it was such a pain in the ass to get to, with lots of deadfalls and steep terrain.

We volunteered to go in the late afternoon to search for the deer, following a scant blood trail that she had tracked for a while before getting fatigued and intimidated by the terrain. Because both my grandfather and I were in good shape and he was so familiar, it didn't seem like a big deal. Before we left, she mentioned hearing what she assumed were coyotes which made her even more so concerned that if the deer died they would ruin the meat and hide before she could harvest it.

We took off in the early evening, expecting to be back within an hour or two after searching and having our guns with us in case we found the animal still alive or came across another buck worth trying to harvest. It was steep in places, with lots and lots of deadfall of varying heights making the hike slower and more tedious than we had hoped, making us understand the other hunter's fatigue. She had marked the blood trail with bright orange pieces on the trees which we followed for maybe 20 minutes and then it got hard to track. The sun was getting close to setting at this point and we knew getting out would be just as long as getting in. We had just about decided to stop when we found a spot near a fallen tree that looked like it had been recently bedded down in, followed by splatters of fairly fresh blood and we continued for longer.

When the sun had just about set and the light had faded from the trees, we removed the firing caps from our guns to make them now completely safe as it was now illegal and irresponsible to hunt in such absence of decent light. My grandfather pulled out his large Maglite flashlight from his pack and I put on my headlamp to begin the hike back, using our GPS to find the trailhead.

About ten minutes on the way back, we started to hear more movement among the trees. It was normal for animals to start moving now that the sun had gone down as animals would likely be starting to head towards clearings for water or to graze in the safety of lower light. Small and distant sounds of crunching leaves, patterings of hooved animals, or small bits of movement in the trees from squirrels or birds were common and expected. We did not expect the deafening, disturbing sound we heard next, which vaguely and initially

reminded me of a coyote howl but by a few seconds in it was uniden-
tifiable, frightening, and human-like.

It started with what sounded like a person screaming but then got
louder and more intense, with a screech to it; so unlike any coyote or
any animal we had ever heard. Then was the almost chittering that
came in between the shrieks and the movement of the trees
becoming almost calculated... almost threatening.

We stopped dead in our tracks; frozen as my grandfather started
using the light to look around. I was far more freaked out than him at
this point. He just seemed perplexed, curious, and a little baffled at
what could make that sound. It sounded human but with no words,
with no urge of tone of "help" or "I'm just screaming to mess with
you." We continued on after it mostly stopped and it seemed like the
other natural and distant sounds had gone almost silent. I listened
intently to the sound of my boots crunching with the dry aspen leaves
underfoot, trying to tell myself that it was just some weird coyote with
a horribly deformed larynx or something.

Maybe 20 minutes from the main trail that would lead us to the
truck, we heard the chittering sound again and [the] sounds of
thumping against dead trees. Looking around with our lights, in
between deadfall maybe 12 - 15 feet in front of us was a large human-
looking thing. It was almost hunched down with a long, slender arm
around the front of a standing aspen. The aspen of course was pale
white with the knots being dark brown and whatever it was had skin
almost as pale. I caught a very brief glimpse of its face. It seemed round
and the eyes seemed sunken and I could not tell you eye color other
than a flash of reflection on the eye from my light and that its face
seemed sunken and emaciated. I didn't see any fur or hair. I never felt
like it looked right at me, more at my grandfather and just in our direction, almost confused and curious like he was before with the sound.

For a mere couple of seconds, I caught a glimpse of it but that was
it. I looked down at the ground holding my eyes shut tight trying to
imagine being safe and secure in the truck and my grandfather took a
few stumbling steps backward toward me. I heard the thing go off to

our side, moving quickly and with purpose through the trees, to the side, and then dropped down behind us (I would assume according to the sound) but I hope it went in the opposite direction. My grandfather turned to where it had veered off as to follow it, but he soon stopped and looked at me. I had never before and never since seen him so confused, baffled, horrified, curious, and in awe. I was crying at this point, ugly crying, trying to muffle my shaking breath and voice and I asked him, "What was that?"

Over and over I asked and he had no answer for me. He pulled his gun off his shoulder sling and put a cap back on the nipple of the igniter, making the gun live and he then carried it in front of his body in his arm. He pulled out another headlight to put on himself. We started walking again towards the trail as he listed off things, talking to himself as to what it wasn't; things like, "Couldn't of been a deer or elk or moose. It had arms, it was hunched, it stood upright," or, "A bear? A very sick bear? It could've been a bear. Was it the light?"

We heard the sound, the screeching human howl, distantly once more before reaching the trail which was dirt and gravel but fairly flat and no deadfall. We practically jogged to the truck. I locked the doors immediately and sobbed and my grandfather turned on music as loud as possible to try to distract me on the way back to camp. I was a mess when we arrived back and he went to talk with the others by the fire when he got me settled in my sleeping bag in my bunk. He explained some to his friends but I don't know what all was said.

The next day everyone was extra sweet to me, trying to comfort me and saying it was probably a sick animal that looked scary in the dark. The deer the hunter shot was found the next day in the daylight, scavenged quite harshly by what I assume were coyotes.

To this day he has no clue what it was, nor what that sound was, and before and since I've heard both coyote and many other animal sounds that never even compared to that sound. The scientist in me, and in him, the hopeful and blissfully ignorant people in us hope and speculate it was just a deformed, sick animal in scant light but I still have no clue of what that thing was and I hope I never ever experience it again."

Eyewitness sketch provided by Ms. Nielsen.

Follow up dialogue

<u>NB</u>: What has your grandfather said about it?

<u>SN</u>: Recently, not much. When I asked about it last time he seemed shaken and he told me it still really bothers him that he can't figure out what it was. He's talked about the possibility of it being a near-death black bear with mange but he even discredits that theory. He initially tried to say that the sounds were crazy coyote calls but after seeing the thing and it making the sounds right by us he has agreed that it wasn't coyotes. He's the kind of guy that just doesn't get shaken and scared but that night he was the most terrified I've ever seen him. If he had truly thought it was a bear he would've hollered

and yelled at it to scare it off like you're supposed to, but he didn't. I did tell him a couple of days after it happened that I think it was crazy of him to take a couple of steps toward it as it started to take off like if he was going to follow it out of curiosity. I don't understand that, not even a little bit.

For a second there it seemed like he was going to try to follow it. Screw that. Nope. Never. If I wasn't scared to the point of being almost frozen in fear I would've screamed and run away as fast as possible. It scares me to think of what might have happened if he decided to try to follow it.

14

NATHANIEL TRUMAN

NAME OF EYEWITNESS	Nathaniel Truman
DATE/TIME OF SIGHTING	"Around Christmas," 2015. Between the 11th and 20th.
LOCATION OF SIGHTING	Moreland Hills, Cleveland, Ohio.
CIRCUMSTANCES PRIOR TO SIGHTING	Driving back from a movie.
NOTABLE SIGHTING DETAILS	Small, large-headed creature with short limbs.

Initial statement

"I'm an Australian but have family in the states. Four years ago, in December 2015, I was in Ohio for Christmas staying with my sister. My sister, her husband (we'll call him Jordan), and I were driving back to her house from a movie and were pulling into her driveway when we heard a high pitch screeching sound come from outside (away from the car). Assuming it was a bat or something, we all got out thinking nothing of it but then we heard it again. It was around the time the sun was setting but the noise was too low to the ground to be a bat. It sounded like it was coming from pretty close by.

Now, the noise wasn't unbearably loud or anything but it was uncomfortably high pitched, like higher than anything I've ever heard. So by this point, we're all out of the car. We hear it, like, one more time before Jordan goes over to the side of the house where he thinks the noise is coming from. He kicks some bricks around and picks up a couple of tiles before we see it.

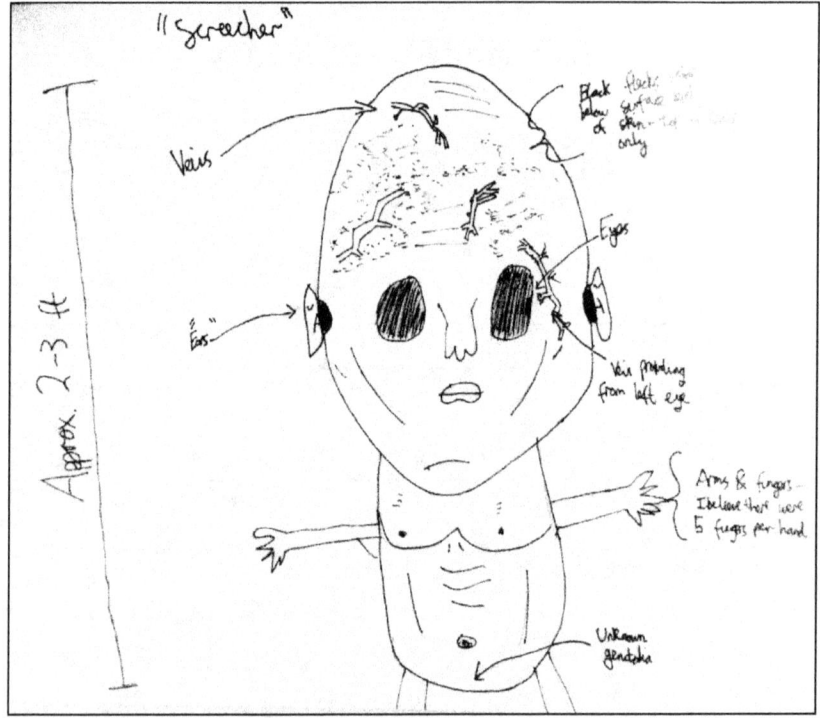

Eyewitness sketch provided by Mr. Truman.

Please understand, the following description may be slightly inaccurate as it has been four years but I swear that what I saw was actually there, both my sister and her husband saw the same thing:

It was vaguely humanoid. It was only about 2-3 feet tall, stark naked, bipedal, running away from Jordan towards us. Its head was massive compared to its body and was semi-translucent; you could see big veins all over it. It had beady black eyes and I didn't get a chance to see if it had any genitalia.

Upon approaching us, my sister screamed, I instinctively jumped back and it changed course and ran onto the road. It ran behind the house across the road, let out another screech, and that was the last we saw of it. Jordan called the police when we got inside. They didn't believe us. All three of us remember the event quite vividly."

Follow up dialogue

NB: How exaggerated would you say the features are in the sketch to what you actually saw?

NT: Well like I said, I'm not exactly an artist. It's difficult to quantify how exaggerated this kind of thing is but in my mind, that's what I saw. It's been a few years but if you put a gun to my head, that's what I would draw.

NB: What are the black dots on the head?

NT: The top layer of skin on its head appeared to be slightly translucent. Those dark specks were visible underneath the skin. As for what they are, I'm not too sure. It's been suggested that I might've seen a baby owl. To address this, I looked up various images and videos of various baby owl species and I can quite confidently say the thing that I saw does not match in appearance or behaviour. That's not to totally rule it out as an option, it has been four years after all. I'll contact my sister and see if she has a different opinion but at this point in time I don't think a baby owl is a match.

15

PRIVATE JACK RYMANOWSKI

NAME OF EYEWITNESS	Private Jack Rymanowski
DATE/TIME OF SIGHTING	First week of January 2016 at approximately 1:30 p.m.
LOCATION OF SIGHTING	Just outside Minneapolis, Minnesota.
CIRCUMSTANCES PRIOR TO SIGHTING	Walking dogs through golf course/forest.
NOTABLE SIGHTING DETAILS	Creature seen standing in a tree. Followed eyewitness home. Eyewitness believed it to be a "Wendigo."

Initial statement

"I'm a mortar infantryman for the army. We're trained to deal with deadly situations and be prepared to fight to the death if needed. My experience happened approximately four years ago but he hasn't left me alone since then.

One day during January, my parents had me walk the family dog and my dog so I decided to bring them to the golf course that was shut down for the season.

Now across the golf course, there's a small forest area that I usually walked them in because it's the closest I get to forests since I live in the city. I live about 20 minutes from Minneapolis, Minnesota. It's very industrialized here and it's one place you wouldn't expect to run into something like this. I went in through the opening and went down the trail. That place always felt like it was really off for some reason; I don't know, call it a sense that something is wrong with that place and the fact that there's no sound in the woods. I ignored it and went on with their walk. Suddenly, I felt like I was being watched. I couldn't tell anything with all the snow on the trees and the fact that there was no snow that fell from them either. So like a dumbass, I ignored it and went on.

I went out to the other side of the forest and headed up a hill that led to a road that leads to the end of the golf course. I felt the feeling of being watched again and turned around on instinct and saw it. It was a pale white figure standing in the tree. I'm a person who always believed in the supernatural and enjoyed studying it and I knew what that thing was. It was a Wendigo and I knew I needed to get out of there. For those who don't know, a Wendigo is a mythical creature in Native American folklore. It's believed to be a carnivorous monster that never stops eating.

I ran as fast as I could with the dogs across the street and it started to chase me and I almost got hit by an oncoming van. He stopped and looked at what I was running from and immediately got back in his van and drove off faster than he did before. While it was distracted, I ran as fast as I could and like a dumbass, I ran back to my home.

Once I got home, I acted as naturally as I could and went to my room and tried my best to calm down and by dinner, I had calmed down enough to eat. Once it came to going to bed, it's when it started to get creepy. To explain the layout of where I am in the house, my room is right below the roof and has another small roof that is above the front porch which is right outside my window. I shut my blinds and got ready for bed but then I heard footsteps on my roof followed by a small thump right outside my window. I saw the silhouette of it. That f--ker was hunched over looking in my window as if he could see me. I was terrified by this and couldn't sleep at all. I couldn't even breathe. It stood there for what felt like an eternity which was only about two hours. After that time had passed he gave up after letting out a scream. It was like a mix of the <u>Alien</u> scream and a cat getting skinned alive. My parents wondered what was going on and I made up some bulls--t excuse. They believed me and headed back to bed. There was no need to get them into this and it's not like they'd believe me anyway. My dumba-- didn't take a picture or video.

That wasn't the end of it. This happened every day of every week for about two months then turned to every other day to every week to every month. Nowadays I don't see it much but I see it every now and then.

If you ever run into a Wendigo: Run; Run as fast as you can, as far away as you can. I don't care if you have to run to a new city, f--k, I don't care if you have to leave the state, just run so far away that you lose that f--ker or the same events that happened to me may happen to you. Be careful, sometimes while searching for monsters they'll end up finding you."

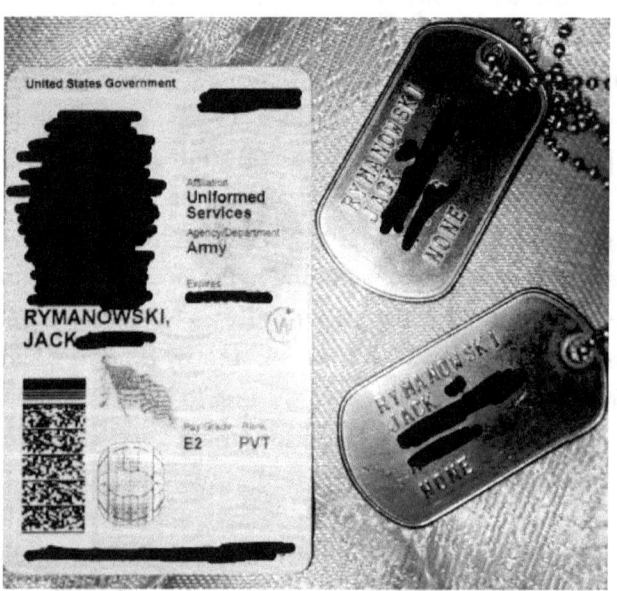

Private Rymanowski's evidence of his military status.

Follow up dialogue

NB: Can you describe what it looked like in more detail?

JR: "He was pale. Like ashes. His eyes were black and looked as if they went on forever. If I had to guess his height it would be from 6 – 7 ft. tall. His head was like a human's but it was different. He had no lips and all that was shown were sharp teeth. His arms were longer than they were supposed to be, I think they were down to his knees. He had claws where his nails were supposed to be. I have an encounter with a Skinwalker. Not nearly as long but in the same place roughly."

NB: I'd love to hear about it.

JR: "It was after my Wendigo encounter in 2016. My dog had died. In 2018, I was 18 and was told by MEPS I would be going to infantry school in Fort Benning, Georgia in 2019. I was told by my parents to walk the family dog. He's an 80 lb. purebred chocolate lab named Cocoa. I decided to go to the same area I usually went as I haven't seen anything different. My roommate was there when I found the first sign of evidence. We traveled to one of the ponds that were on the course and I found a weird set of tracks. They were large bird tracks that then slowly morphed into dog or coyote tracks. I asked my roommate about it and he didn't know. I only had a small amount of data about this but it matched up with a Skinwalker. The tracks changing in the snow to a different animal was the first sign and I didn't want to stick around and find a 150 lb. coyote around. We headed back to my house and we didn't speak of this again.

The following day I went out to the same place but this time I saw something in the distance. It looked human from the start but as I got closer I knew what it was as I watched it slowly turn into a wolf. I didn't want to make any sudden movements. The dog was scared shit-less and lying helplessly next to me. I waited until it went away but it didn't. It's like he knew I was there. About ten minutes passed and he headed to the woods patch that was across the street. I decided to use the opportunity to run home. I never saw him again. I still go to that patch of woods and went there in 2019 with my fiancé and family dog and saw nothing. It's weird as when I'm there alone I find things but when I'm accompanied I don't."

NB: "Would there be any way to confirm your military status? I'd love to include an official photograph or something for the report."

JR: "Yes, I'll be able to tell you my current unit: 1-194 HHC, combined arms regiment. Mechanized Mortar Infantry. If you need paperwork I can send you it or a shot of my Military ID but there will need to be censorship because of privacy."

16

"JAKE" (ALIAS)

NAME OF EYEWITNESS	"Jake" (alias)
DATE/TIME OF SIGHTING	Between Easter and the beginning of May 2017.
LOCATION OF SIGHTING	Pilot Mountain, North Carolina.
CIRCUMSTANCES PRIOR TO SIGHTING	Taking the dog outside.
NOTABLE SIGHTING DETAILS	History of sightings in the area. Possible supernatural implications.

Initial report

"I'll preface this by saying that I'm a big believer in the paranormal; I used to find it laughable but wound up living in a violently haunted house, for more than a decade, which opened my mind up a fair bit. That being said, I still generally assume that most creepy encounters (including my own) are misidentifications unless something suggests otherwise.

But anyway, about two years ago I got saddled with taking care of a puppy. He was only about six weeks old at the time so he required a crap-load of attention and care, the most annoying of which was that he had to be taken outside to pee every two hours or so even (often especially) in the middle of the night or else you had a mess on your hands.

Now stumbling outside half awake at 3 a.m. in the freezing cold is disorienting at the best of times but the trailer I've been renting (in rural NC for the record) has a bit of a disturbing history* that makes every little sound or shadow feel a little more sinister than it is.

*(No idea what actually happened, literally nobody does, but about six months before I started renting the place one of the tenants disappeared from his bed in the middle of the night and was found torn to shreds about 200 yards away in the thickest part of the woods, lying in a small creek about two months later. He'd been ranting about demonic possession and that 'they' were coming for him for months prior and although he was obviously partially eaten they couldn't figure out what did it. This sounds a little over the top but it's assumed he was an undiagnosed schizophrenic that wandered off drunk. Coyotes are everywhere around here, as are black bears, and although there aren't supposed to be cougars in the area we aren't too far from the mountains and a fair handful of neighbors say they think they've heard one prowling.)

It was one of these nights that my little buddy woke me up squalling to pee and I stumbled down the steps to let him do his business. He immediately started crying to go back inside, his bladder still full, and I had to chase him up the steps a couple of times; getting increasingly irritated the whole time. After about the fourth time I placed him in the grass he couldn't hold it anymore and I looked around to give him some privacy. That's when I saw... something.

It was peering over my neighbor's hedge at us, standing upright and seemingly about to crawl over until it was spotted. I didn't have my glasses on, so I can't really speak to specific details but whatever it was was ridiculously white, rail thin, obviously naked and had unnervingly long arms. The hedge is around 6 ft. and it could just see over, so I'd estimate it was around the same height.

When I looked at it, it stood stock still in the darkness but when I turned my flashlight on it dropped back on the neighbor's side and scurried on all fours around the side of her house and out of sight. My blood ran cold and I slept in the living room that night because my bedroom was on the same side of the house that I saw that thing and had a large unobstructed window that I just didn't feel like sitting in front of for a few days.

I mentioned it to some other people in the house and they laughed it off as me imagining things, seeing the neighbor's cat, or even her meth-head daughter streaking but it just didn't come up again for a good long while. I figured maybe it was just my imagination running wild.

A few months ago I got married and now we have three dogs that have to be taken out before we can go to sleep. They're three goofy, high-energy, extremely protective Pitbulls that always seem super excited. Off and on I had to spend the night at my sister's house to put my nieces on the bus so she could go into work early so my wife had to take the dogs out before going to sleep by herself. Several times she's mentioned the dogs whining and wanting to go in without using the bathroom, hearing something fairly large crawling around in the woods, seeing weird eyeshine in the brush that runs off when her light hits it, and hearing a strange sound she could only describe as 'chittering.'

I was trying to find a sound that matched what she was talking about to try and set her mind at ease when some variation on the phrase 'chittering in woods' led to a story on Fleshgaits. I rolled my eyes at the typical Creepypasta BS, but the obviously fake picture included made my skin crawl and my heart pound because it was EXACTLY the way I remember that night. Literally hadn't thought of it in two years but hearing so many people describe the exact same thing recently makes me think that maybe I shouldn't have dismissed it so easily."

<u>Follow up dialogue</u>

"The sightings that my dad mentioned were some time in the last month or so (September 2019) but he's out this way so often he isn't sure exactly when.

I assume you're looking for the date of the missing tenant but I don't have a lot of personal information on that. I want to say that I moved here in the summer of 2015 and that from what I've gathered his family officially moved out around a month before I showed up. I BELIEVE he'd been found a month or so before that.

I find the subject interesting myself so I'm glad to help. I didn't mention this in the thread because it didn't seem pertinent, but twice since I've lived here (and since the sighting) I've heard what sounds like something MASSIVE crashing through the woods in our direction when we got too close to the brush. Could be anything from a deer or even a bear, to local rednecks acting like assholes but I will say that my dad hacked his way into the brush a few days later to see if he could find tracks and found a bunch of sizable branches broken around 6 - 8 feet off the ground and stacked into teepee formations. I'll point out that my dad isn't exactly an impartial observer however as he's a Bigfoot enthusiast that was hoping to find something like what he found. Doubt if it's related, but thought it was interesting enough to mention all the same. If you're focusing on humanoids then you might want to check out NC in general though. I don't have any more firsthand cryptid experience than I've already mentioned but I've heard numerous second (or in some cases third or fourth) hand stories of Goatmen, leprechauns, Bigfoot, and Dogmen over the years. Can't say I'd put much stock in most of the sources but a few were from guys not known to bulls--t.

I can't say if this is real or just the ravings of a lonely drunk, but when I was a kid my dad had a friend that claimed to speak with 'leprechauns' in the woods behind his house. He described them as between two and three feet tall with leathery skin and needle-like teeth. He claimed that they would leave neon green globs of phlegm filled with four-leaf clovers all over his house and car. People always joked about him but his four-year-old daughter would talk about them too and people who stayed at his house would find the weird little phlegm balls. He told my dad once that he could show them to him if he wanted to see them but that for his own safety, he wasn't allowed to take a gun or knife into the woods with him. My dad being the kind of guy that keeps a .44 next to the toilet, just in case someone breaks in while he's pooping, declined the offer. I wish I knew how to get in touch with the guy, because I'd love to pick his brain as an adult, but he's sort of lost touch with his old friends over the years."

17

JAKY & NICK CORRELL AND OTHER

NAME OF EYEWITNESS	Jaky & Nick Correll and other.
DATE/TIME OF SIGHTING	May 28th, 2017.
LOCATION OF SIGHTING	Red River Gorge, Kentucky.
CIRCUMSTANCES PRIOR TO SIGHTING	Hiking at night.
NOTABLE SIGHTING DETAILS	Extensive encounters and interactions including several eyewitnesses.

Initial statement

"Okay, so I have no idea what we saw exactly that night. I have searched everywhere for sightings or even myths around the area we saw it and have found nothing. If anyone has any idea what we saw or even if anyone else has seen it please let me know. My husband and I think it could be a Wendigo but I don't know. I haven't heard anyone else say they've seen anything like it in RRG. I guess I want help figuring out what we saw and what to do. After the night I'm about to describe but I think we've had some close encounters with it since.

My friends and I go camping a lot and my favorite place is in Red

River Gorge, Kentucky. We go there often and I've been ever since I was an infant. I'm 28 now, married, with a kid, and still going. It is the closest place to where I live where you can see the Milky Way pretty much every night. It's perfect for stargazing and I've seen a shooting star every clear night I've been there. When we go without our kid we will night-hike to a good lookout point and stargaze for hours.

Our first experiences night-hiking we would go to trails we knew well and were used frequently during the day. Ones with log fences and gazebo resting places. The most used trail is a trail in Natural Bridge State Park that leads up to the 'natural bridge.' This trail is around two miles uphill depending on your starting point. I've done this trail every summer of my life and could do it blindfolded. It has wooden steps, carved rock steps, log handrails, multiple sitting points under a roof, trash cans, but after reaching the main trailhead it has no lights at all. It's used often and while it is uphill the difficulty is low. As long as you have good grip on your shoes and water you'll be fine. My friends have done it with me multiple times and are confident in it as well. Hiking this trail at night is not allowed but it's the woods and I've never really been one to care about closing times for the literal outside.

When we used this main trail to hike to the top we would park in a lot designated for the pool and hoedown island. You walk across the road that leads to the pool and you're at the first trail marker. You go up gravel for a while and pass the Natural Bridge State Park lodge. There's a waterfall and some lights so it was best to go fast and watch out for rangers that would tell us to leave. Then you walk across another road and there's a mini shelter to sit in or a small rock wall to rest your legs. Then it's the beginning of the trail to the top.

The night was weird, to begin with. As soon as we started the hike the clouds took over and it appeared we'd be walking for nothing to even stargaze at but we went anyways, just in case it cleared out by the time we got up there. In the beginning, it was just normal paranoia that was keeping us stressed and quiet it seemed.

You know you've reached the bottom of the bridge when you see a giant wall of limestone. During this time there was a gazebo that was set to the right of this wall and the trail continued and followed next to the wall. Where you come from is a fairly steep part of the trail and the gazebo is welcomed. My husband, my best friend at the time, and I all sat on the gazebo steps (the bench is under a roof and even darker than the rest of outside so we just stayed on the steps) facing where we are looking down the trail that follows the limestone wall. We each have a bright LED headlamp and a handheld flashlight. We don't usually look at each other when we night-hike because the lights are so bright. We sit in a line like in The Lord's Supper and walk in a line or staggered so we don't blind ourselves.

It is after hours at this point. No ski lift rides had gone on for hours and the rangers had already done their sweep and left right before we got out of the car and headed up. We left no time between them making sure the trail and top were clear and us starting our hike up. The ski lift takes you up the top but there are workers that stay and do counts and only leave after it's clear. I guess I have to make these points because that's what I was thinking when what seemed out of nowhere a girl with a headlamp begins to walk down the trail we are looking out at. She is in a sundress and flip-flops. This hike is uphill and while it is a fairly easy hike it is not easy with no water or real shoes. She'd have to have hiked up and down to this point with no food or water. Her light was bright and when she reached where the trail turns from in front of the gazebo to down where we came from she stopped. She just stood there straight on like how a human is presented in an anatomical drawing. She was looking directly at us all sitting there and her light made me bring my hand up to shield my eyes. She didn't turn away from our lights at all, or even seem bothered; she had 6 LED lights aimed directly at her face.

I said, "Hello." She said kind of with a pause between every word something like, "Hello, how, are, you." I said something like, "Good, how are you?" and she took even longer pauses and said, "Oh... I'm... fine." She then just stood there still with her hands at her side and facing and staring at us. Her light made it impossible to really see her face and it was so bright I had my hand up the entire time until she just turned and walked slowly down the trail part we had just come up. She got to a part where the trail turned and we saw her light just stay in that one spot for a minute until she turned and the light faded out of sight.

We wait for a while before continuing up. I kept making comments about how weird that was and everyone else just made it out to be me always being afraid but no one ever came after her. She had done this hike alone. At night? And somehow without being found by any ranger?

We got up after a bit and started back up to the top. It felt like it took much longer than it ever had in the past but we made it to the top. There's stone steps named 'Fat Man Squeeze' that get you to the top of the bridge and you can walk across it and whatever.

Going up and being on the top we could hear twigs snapping, almost alternating from the left then the right. We lay down and try to stargaze but the clouds are even thicker now. It was miserably hot. We could hear voices at times and my husband kept checking for people we heard. He never saw anyone. We saw a light flash. Never saw anyone attached to it and then we heard a bird call? But it wasn't like a real bird noise at all. It sounded like a person making bird calls, like rhythmic and not really natural? I was convinced we weren't alone and hadn't been alone but also I am the most easily spooked. I asked to leave as soon as they were ready to and they were ready right then and there and that scared me: that they were just as afraid as me at this point.

We began going down the way we came and it felt like it was taking so long. We were going steady and quick and it was downhill but we were not making any ground it seemed. It's hard to explain but it was so weird that at one point I even said it out loud. I said, "This feels much longer," and they agreed with me. I kept looking behind me with the flashlight and my husband kept looking out to the sides and my friend kept hers mostly forward.

I kept feeling watched and couldn't figure out what footsteps were ours or if they were all ours that I heard. I would turn in the direction of any noise but not see anything. When my husband was walking he kept saying he was catching eyes in his flashlight. Usually, you can catch raccoon eyes spying on you or some animal like that. He was afraid maybe a bear or big dog or something and he never got his lights on whatever eyes they were long enough to see an animal's size or shape.

Now we're hiking down a semi-flattish area, compared to the downhill hike we've been doing at least. The log fence or handrail or whatever it's called is on our right side. We are in a row walking within reaching distance of this barrier and my husband just stops walking altogether and says, "What's that?" but the question is more like an alert and I move my hand lamp in that direction and don't see anything at first.

Then both of his lights catch a shape and then my headlamp catches it and I move my hand lamp to [the] center and catch it while my friend simultaneously finds it in her lights as well. All six lights shine onto, and kind of reflect off of, a light-gray creature. It is bent in a crouching position kneeling on its right leg and starts turning towards us. It starts to slowly stand and my mind is racing still. It looks human but it is too big. People mistake human shapes for what's actually bears in the woods often but this is skinny. It is thin and big and almost white. It's so light gray and its skin resembles dolphin skin. There's a shine to it and our lights get reflected a little when they're on it. It gradually comes to a full standing position in front of us. Its head is long and its eyes are in a human position on the face in front and not on the side like animals but I could not see any other facial features. Just big almost empty holes or pits that were its eyes. It looked directly at us and our lights. The way it stood was intimidating, almost like when a snake raises up and flexes their necks all crazy to show prey that they're stronger and smarter. It was like it was stepping up to a fight, from crouching, then turning, then standing front-on in front of us. The arms hung down low and the hands seemed long too. Its hands had to be by its knees? I'd guess it stood 9 ft. or so and not that far in front of us. No hair at all and its head was large as well. I couldn't process what I saw and was frozen.

Then I just feel my husband hitting me on the back and yelling, "Run. Run. Run."

I start to understand we have to get away from this thing and it pivots and runs to the right. Going backward on the trail so it could get around the barrier and onto the trail behind us. We take off running the rest of the way down the trail. Knowing that this thing just took off much faster than us and after it had crossed from behind the barrier, it would be gaining on us quick. We didn't talk at all because when we tried it felt almost like we would get caught. We keep running as fast as we can but some areas are so steep. It never felt like we were out of sight from this creature.

As we made it to the trail beginning with the gravel we could hear something to the side crashing down through the forest. We ran until we got to the car and then we drove as fast as we could and as soon as we got to the main road the sky cleared up and the stars were out.

When that thing looked at us I knew it was smarter and faster than us. I knew that if we hadn't seen it that it could have easily taken one of us and gotten away. I think the only reason it hesitated was because so many of us saw it at once and we stayed together.

When we made it back to where we were staying all of us took out our phones and wrote a note [about] what we saw happen. We hadn't spoken about it until after we looked at each other's phones and the stories were the same. Without a doubt, we had all seen something real."

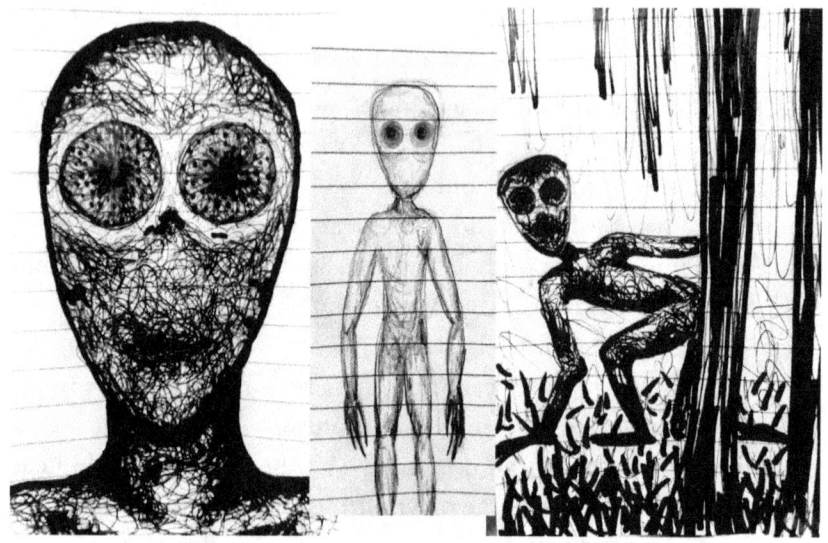

The very first sketches created by Ms. Correll of what she and her group had seen.

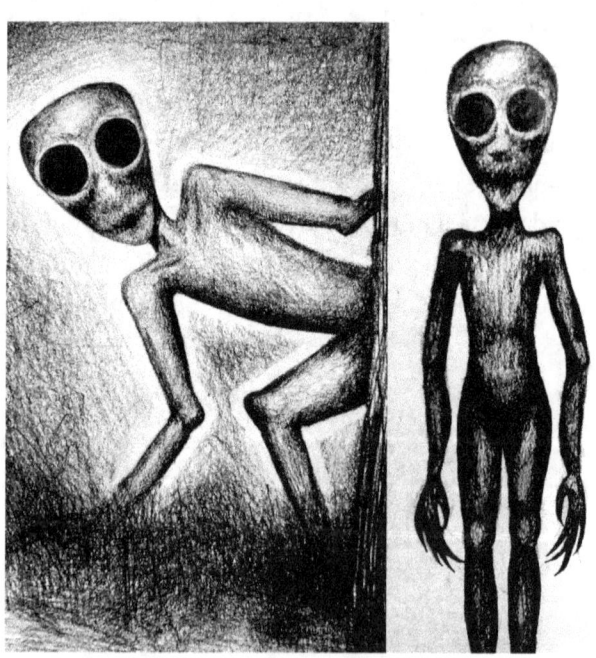

Updated sketches by Ms. Correll. The most recent updated art by Ms. Correll.

18

LOGAN H.

NAME OF EYEWITNESS	Logan ███████
DATE/TIME OF SIGHTING	October 2017 (the week before Halloween; the 25th or 26th).
LOCATION OF SIGHTING	Chanhassen, Minnesota.
CIRCUMSTANCES PRIOR TO SIGHTING	Biking home from work.
NOTABLE SIGHTING DETAILS	Inexplicable scent of blueberry pie.

Initial statement

"**B**ack in 2017, I used to live with my aunt in Minnesota and while living with her I had worked at the nearby Walgreens which was about a 35-40 minute bike ride from her place. This event happened in October, eerily enough. One night, I worked the closing shift but we didn't close and leave 'til about 30-40 minutes longer than what we used to due to lots of work needing to be done. I biked to and from work, so as someone who believes in the paranormal stuff 100% biking home at night was always an eerie thing to do because my mind would often go wild.

Now, the route I take to go home is a somewhat isolated one; I have to go past a park and a lot of wooded areas and it's barely lit up as there aren't many street lights or houses for most of that route. I had just gotten to the park area where it's more nature-y and woodsy. I was talking to an ex on the phone (who was currently my girlfriend at the time) as a way to ease my nerves on the way home. I had briefly looked down at my phone when I heard a weird screeching sound which caused me to look up.

There, to my horror, was this large, tall, deathly frail-looking humanoid creature that looked very white and pale; almost as if it was sickly. Before I could really get a good look at it, it dropped onto all fours and leaped into the wooded area. Seeing this, I panicked and began to pedal as fast as I could. Meanwhile, I could hear the thing taking chase but remaining hidden in the woods. I could hear branches constantly snapping, and leaves crunching. This thing was in pursuit.

I got about halfway through the route, to a point where nature stops being trees and woods and opens up into a rolling hills sort of thing, just flat grass but a bunch of hills. As soon as I got to this point, I heard the thing stop chasing me and complete silence. That's when I noticed a very peculiar scent: blueberry pie, which really weirded me out because there are no houses, restaurants, or buildings of any kind around this area so for the scent of a freshly baked blueberry pie (my favorite pie) really seemed sketchy.

I paid no attention to it, as to me it was coming from the distant hills as if this thing was somehow creating the scent to draw me away from the sidewalk and towards it. So I kept pedaling and eventually made it to where the townhomes were and eventually back home to safety which, yes, yes I did throw my bike into the garage and run inside and up to my bedroom like a frightened child and turn on the light and TV.

Now, it doesn't end there. A few days later on Halloween when I started forgetting about the thing I saw, I spent the day handing out candy for my aunt and watching TV/YouTube until it was time to retire to the bedroom. Shortly after I had gone to my room I, again, heard that weird screeching sound and for some reason, my idiot self decided to check out the window. There, about 40 - 50 ft. away from the house standing underneath a few trees, was the creature/thing which made me quickly close the window and shut the blinds.

The next day, surprisingly, my aunt asked me if I had heard the sound last night and seen the thing as well. I guess from what she had told me she had heard the noise and wanted to see what it was so she took the dog and went into the backyard and had seen the thing standing there, then [it] almost immediately drop to all fours and leap away. Now when it comes to this thing's size I'd say when I saw it standing on two feet it was about 7 - 8 ft. tall (I'm 6 ft. 7 in. tall) so it was quite taller than me. It looked very pale, like it was nothing but skin and bones, yet moved incredibly fast from the speed it had lept away and pursued me while I was biking home."

Original sketch provided by the eyewitness.

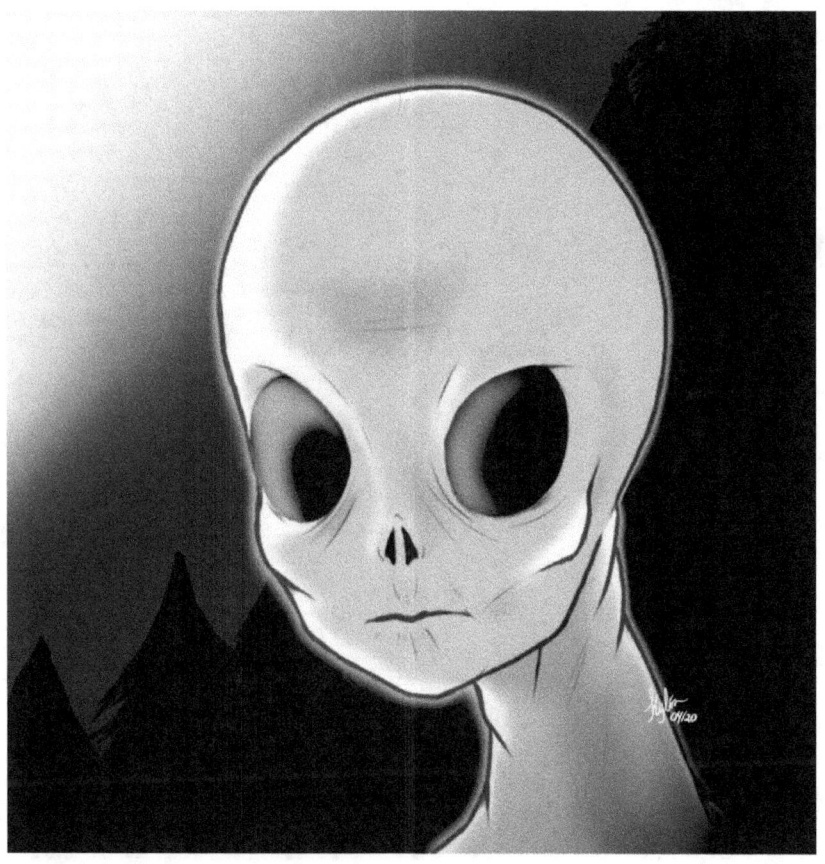

Refined eyewitness sketch by Kylira Brown (@Chibi_Pichu).

19

DAVID FRIES II

NAME OF EYEWITNESS	David Fries II
DATE/TIME OF SIGHTING	December 27th, 2017 at approx. 2:30 am
LOCATION OF SIGHTING	Woodlawn Road, Macclenny, Florida.
CIRCUMSTANCES PRIOR TO SIGHTING	Driving home from a friend's house.
NOTABLE SIGHTING DETAILS	Pinkish fleshy skin with long hairs.

Initial statement

"This happened in the north Florida area. So I saw this thing about three years ago. I drew this as soon as I got home. It was after 2 a.m. one night I was on my way home from a friend's. I took a back road home just because it loops around to my part of town. It's a twisty road that earned the nickname 'Snake Road.' This road has no lights, no nothing. Pitch black.

Well as I was coming around one of the curves, I was going the speed limit at 45 mph maybe even 50 because who doesn't like a thrill when taking a curve? As I turned the curve going right, on the small strip of road before the turn going left, I saw it. It was crouched on the side of the road in the grass but not far from the pavement. It was hunched over and moving as if it were eating or maybe digging, I'm not sure, but I was able to see another one farther down in the ditch as I passed by. It didn't even turn around or flinch when a Nissan Sentra with its brights on blared around the corner pushing 50 mph. Granted, I only saw these things for a total of three, maybe four seconds as I passed. I know what I saw.

Call me crazy. I've been big on cryptozoology since I was in high school. I wouldn't make this up. I want to try and understand the unknown but I never thought I'd see something so disturbing and unsettling and it's been on my mind since. I've got theories as to what it could be. Possibly aliens or maybe some kind of dimension hopper or perhaps just an inbred hillbilly that's been locked away for its whole life finally escaped?"

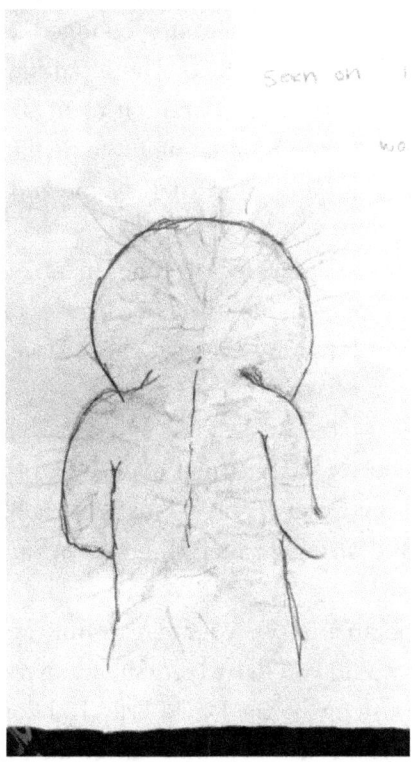

Eyewitness sketch provided by Mr. Fries II.

Follow up dialogue

DF II: I would love nothing more than to help you. I have always wanted to get into cryptozoology and when I saw this thing it only made me want to look for the unknown more. Thank you for reaching out. I'd be more than happy to answer any questions you may have. The drawing of the creature was done by myself as well.

NB: Would you be able to describe the experience in more detail?

DF II: It was on a drive home from my friends, I was coming around a turn on a very twisty road. I was going about 45mph and I had my brights on. The road was pitch black with no streetlights and as I came up on the next turn it was crouched or sitting on the side of the road next to a "soft shoulder" sign.

NB: What was going through your head when you saw it?

DF II: Well as I approached it with my vehicle I wondered what it was and when I got right up next to it, it changed too. "What the hell is that?" I wondered who would be out here pulling a prank like that. Well, as I drove home and thought about it I had all kinds of thoughts going on in my head. When I got home I told my family and immediately started drawing it. They didn't believe me and thought I was on drugs or something.

NB: How would you describe how the skin looked??

DF II: The skin looked smooth, like a hairless mole rat, and the hair was stringy and long and didn't seem to have a purpose in my opinion.

NB: You didn't see a face?

DF II: No, it had its back turned to me, unfortunately. Maybe I was lucky enough not to see its face. I just saw its back and I saw the same pink flesh and stringy hair farther down on the ditch as if it were a second one.

NB: Would I be able to use your name, initials, or a pseudonym for the case file or would you like to remain anonymous?

DF II: You can use my name: David Fries II. I don't mind at all. I'd rather it be known it was me so people can relate to an actual person rather than an anonymous tale, you know what I mean?

20

ELI GAIANI

NAME OF EYEWITNESS	Eli Gaiani
DATE/TIME OF SIGHTING	The week before July 4th, 2018 at approx. 5:30 a.m.
LOCATION OF SIGHTING	South Dakota.
CIRCUMSTANCES PRIOR TO SIGHTING	Awakened by his dog acting aggressively towards something outside.
NOTABLE SIGHTING DETAILS	Unnaturally fast humanoid sighted by former track athlete.

Initial statement

"My dog typically sleeps right around my arm. His head rests on my shoulder so he is facing the window. When I sleep, the back of my head faces the window.

Anyway, it was just nearing 5:30 a.m. The dog wakes me up with extremely aggressive growling at the window. This growling I've only heard when he fights with other dogs. I was roused and I tried to coo him back to sleep. Within a couple seconds, the growling turned into howls and barks. I looked outside the window and my heart rate shot through the roof.

The property line from my house to my neighbors is 60-70 yards. I competed at State for track for the 100 Open, 400, and two relays so I can confirm this creature's speed was shocking. It covered the yard in no less than three seconds. Gray skin, long arms almost down to its knees, an elongated face, and anorexic-looking legs. It ran by swinging its arms like a buffoon. Not a runner's form.

After collecting myself, I burst into my dad's room. I startled him but told him to get outside with me. We briskly got outside with handguns as I tried to explain what I saw. There were no footprints or marks (as whitetail deer are frequently in our yard)."

Eyewitness sketch provided by Mr. Gaiani.

21

ANONYMOUS 7

NAME OF EYEWITNESS	Anonymous.
DATE/TIME OF SIGHTING	July 2018 at approx. 7:30 p.m.
LOCATION OF SIGHTING	Newaygo, Michigan.
CIRCUMSTANCES PRIOR TO SIGHTING	Hitting golf balls into a pasture.
NOTABLE SIGHTING DETAILS	Bizarre vocalizations and wide mouth.

Initial statement

"I lived most of my life, up to the age of 14, in Michigan. We lived in the Saint Joe area if anyone is familiar with the area. Anyways, my grandparents lived in the northern areas of Michigan and we would regularly drive the 4 - 5+ hour drive and go visit them either on the way to our lake house, which was a little farther north, or just to see them. They lived in the middle of nowhere, you know, "25 minutes to town" sort of thing. Both of their neighbors were a mile in each direction and their property is huge. They live in a small trailer in the middle of the property. They have two pastures to each side of the

NATHANIEL BRISLIN

property and in the back, they had miles of trails that would take you through the woods. My grandfather usually used this for hunting.

I was hitting golf balls from the front of the house into the pasture. I hit all my balls and went to go collect them in the pasture. I opened the gate and shut it behind me so none of the dogs could get through and I walked around picking up balls. A couple of them went farther than normal so I had to walk back behind the pasture area and into the wooded area. As I was walking I could hear leaves being crushed but they were a little off from my steps. I kept hearing this weird noise coming from behind me, kind of like a watery sound I guess. It was like someone just got out of the shower and they were dripping wet but this noise kept stopping and starting so I just thought it was the wind blowing water out of the trees.

I found my last ball and turned around to start walking back and I saw something tallish move behind a tree. I could tell it was taller than me but didn't really know what it was. Being from Michigan, we've got our fair share of scary-ass animals that would love to bite into your meaty flesh but this was definitely not a wolf and could not have been a bear (I would have smelt it) so I kind of stood there frozen just looking at the tree and bushes the thing was near.

After a while, the thing started to creep out. It crawled out on its hands and legs. First, I saw its long skinny arms which were followed by its head. It looked up and around and finally looked at me. It crawled the rest of the way out and I could see the thing whole. It had skinny arms like it hadn't eaten in a while. Dark-looking skin that had a shine to it like it was slimy. Its body was just like a mass of flesh. It didn't look to have a stomach or chest, it was just kind of twisted up and malformed. Its legs were just as long and f--ked up looking as its arms and both the thing's feet and hands were elongated. Not massively or anything but you could tell it was longer than your average foot/hand. Its head was the part I have a really hard time pinpointing down: It had eyes, no hair, and a long mouth that wouldn't open. The nose was just two holes and it had a very long exaggerated chin but it kind of looked normal in a way.

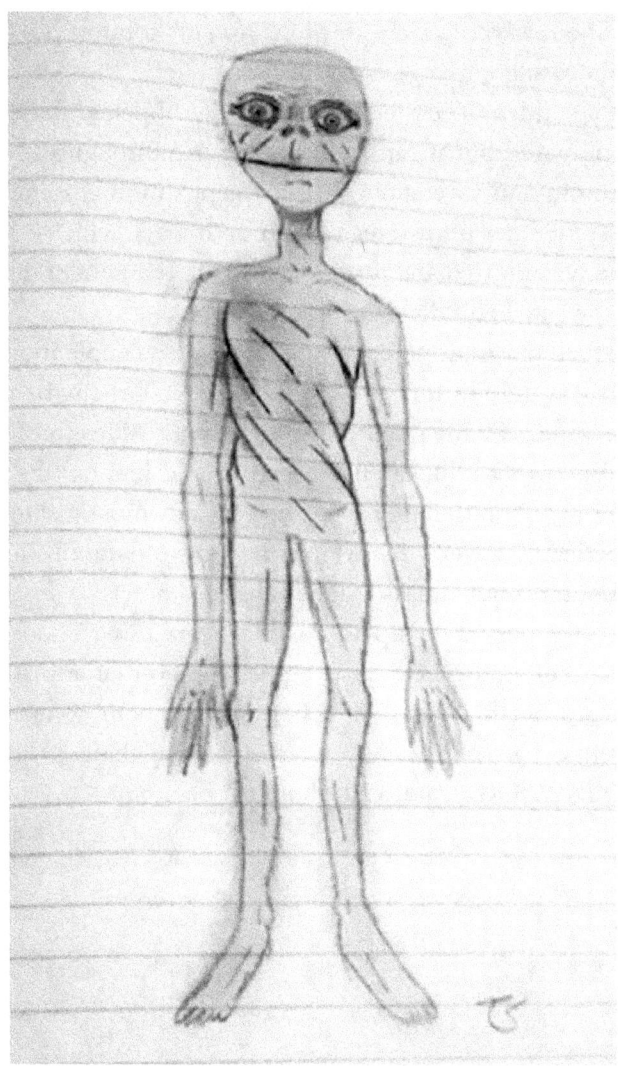

Eyewitness sketch provided by their girlfriend.

It stared at me and without opening its mouth and it made the sounds I had been hearing which seemed to be made by its nose as the holes flared. It started to walk around; not at me but just around where it was. Then it stood up on two legs. It was probably about 6 1/2 ft. tall but its look and appearance made it look a lot scarier. The thing moved its neck in an unnatural way and then it looked at me. It was only about 25 yards away, way too close for comfort but I was not about to move and have this creature charge me.

All of a sudden, it just bolts right at me. I opened my eyes wide and just prepared but it ran right by me and through the woods. I turned around and sure enough, it just kept running, sometimes on all fours, sometimes on two legs. It ran both ways, which was unnatural. Its body contorted and just looked so off. I ran out of the pasture and shut the gate behind me again.

I didn't tell my grandparents right away but a couple months later I did. This was in the summer of 2018. I didn't tell them 'til about the fall of the same year. My grandfather pulled me aside after I told him and asked me what it looked like exactly. I told him and he said he's seen it before out on the trails. He didn't say any more just for me not to be worried. I haven't really told anyone but family and close friends about this but I guess that has changed now.

This really messed me up for a while. Scary thing is too: I've seen it after, several times in different places; never at my home but anywhere up north. Even at a lake cabin an hour away from my grandparents. This one was by far the scariest though. I know it's NOT A SKINWALKER, at least it shouldn't be."

22

ZACH COLVIN

NAME OF EYEWITNESS	Zach Colvin
DATE/TIME OF SIGHTING	Sept. 21st, 2018 at approx. 4:00 a.m.
LOCATION OF SIGHTING	Northern Michigan.
CIRCUMSTANCES PRIOR TO SIGHTING	Walking home from his friend's house.
NOTABLE SIGHTING DETAILS	Visible ears.

Initial statement

"I was walking home from a friend's house late at night, and I didn't expect what I saw...

I was at my grandma's house and got a text from a girl, let's call her Leah. At the time, I kind of liked her. She said that she wanted me to come over because she wanted to take a walk (we live in the country and it's pretty beautiful at night). I checked the time and saw that it was two in the morning. Not a big deal, she only lived two miles down the road. I got up, got dressed, and walked out the door. The walk didn't seem to last too long, so I got to her house quickly. I met her outside and I started off the conversation by saying, "Hey."

"Hey. Took you long enough," she said with a smile.

"Didn't seem like it," I said.

We talked for about five minutes before we started to walk down the road. Out of the blue, she told me to look out for this "thing" that was in the woods. She laughed so I thought she was kidding. A little ways down the road, we stopped to look at a tree that had no bark on one side.

"Probably just a bear," she said. I agreed because bears were common in northern Michigan. After we looped around we came back to her house at about 4:30 a.m.

"I better get going," I said. We both said bye to each other before I started back to my house. I didn't see anything until I was about halfway back. I passed a small barn about 15 ft. wide, 30 ft. long, nothing too big. I didn't pay any attention to it because why would I? If you know what a sliding barn door sounds like you'd know what I heard.

The loud creak filled the open air. I shot around to see what opened it but only saw the darkness of the empty barn. I looked for a second longer. Right before I looked away I saw the bony, clawed hand of whatever the hell that thing was reaching around the barn door frame. I froze in my tracks which wasn't very smart. It stepped out into the moonlight and that's when the color went from my face.

It had huge, glistening eyes and a bony rib cage. Its skin was pale and colorless. It had no nose, just two holes like you'd see on a human skull. It sniffed the air and then immediately turned and looked directly at me. I don't think that I've ever run so fast in my life. I sprinted away from it. I could hear it at my heels. I dare not turn around. I approached an inter-section where two dirt roads met a main road.

I heard the damned thing veer into the brush on the edge of the woods just as I came into the light. I turned around quickly and saw the glistening eyes in the underbrush. It's like they hovered there before disappearing into the darkness of the woods. I was left in silence, the only noise was me trying to catch my breath. I stayed under that light until sun up when I finally had the nerve to head home.

When I got back to my grandma's house she was still asleep. Luckily, I was back right before she woke up. I'm 17 now. It's been 2 years since that horrifying moment and I won't be forgetting it anytime soon."

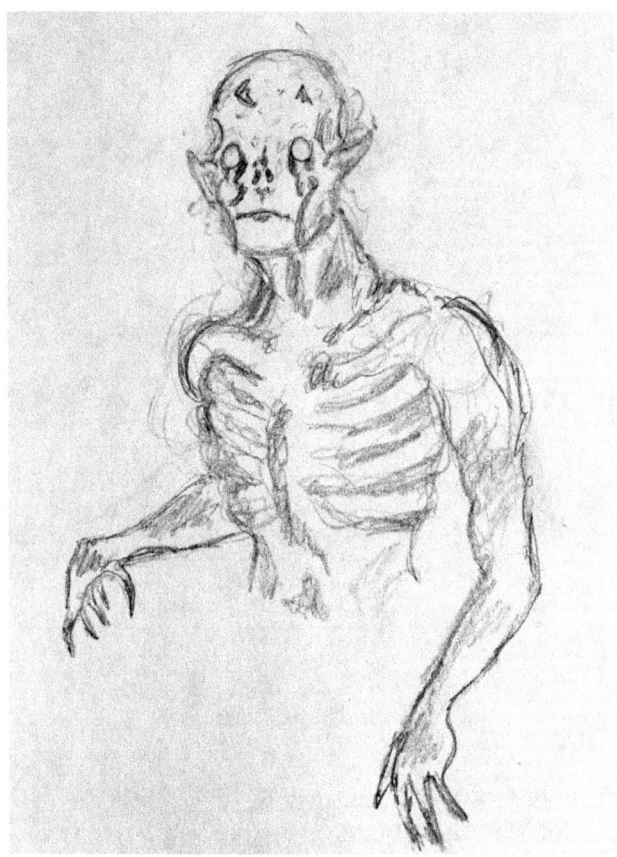

Eyewitness sketch provided by Mr. Colvin.

23

MADI J. AND OTHERS

NAME OF EYEWITNESS	Madi ███████ and others.
DATE/TIME OF SIGHTING	Summer night in 2014 and 2017 as well as a winter night in 2018.
LOCATION OF SIGHTING	Northeastern Missouri.
CIRCUMSTANCES PRIOR TO SIGHTING	Eyewitness was always with friends or family members before sightings.
NOTABLE SIGHTING DETAILS	Three brief nocturnal encounters over the course of four years.

Initial statement

"Hey, I know this might be too late and I'm sure you've gotten lots of messages but I've encountered the same creature multiple times over the past six years. It's a pale, humanoid figure. I remember a lot of them pretty well and I can't give exact dates but I know the years that these incidents happened. They have all happened in northeast Missouri.

The first encounter was in the summer of 2014. I was visiting my uncle's farm to barbecue and have fun with my family. After it got dark we went inside. Later in the night, my stepdad and I walked back outside to do something when I heard some rustling off in the distance. I looked over to see this pale, naked, humanoid creature with big eyes. I froze in fear. Thankfully it ran away across the yard in the direction of the shed with my uncle's tractors where his motion sensor lights turned on. It was the size and shape of a person but it didn't run on all fours like a human would in that position. This thoroughly freaked me out but for some reason, my stepdad missed the whole thing. It happened so fast and whenever I visit that uncle I never go outside alone at night.

Encounter number two was in the summer of 2017. My family and I went camping ███████████████████████ it was set up was you'd rent a lot and you could come any time of the year to spend time there. The lot across the gravel road from ours had been abandoned so nobody was ever there. My parents let my friend come camping too.

So one night, the rest of my family left the lot to go ride on trails through the woods and my friend and I decided to stay behind. She and I were sitting around a campfire when our dog started going crazy. We looked behind us and there it was standing in the other lot. It was one of those nights when the moon was full so you could see everything almost perfectly. My friend and I were absolutely terrified. I think our dog frightened the creature because it walked away as soon as it made itself known. My friend and I hid in the camper until everyone came home.

Now the third encounter is very short but I'll share it anyways. We were driving my cousin home and I was riding with my friend in the winter of 2018. She lived out in the country down a winding blacktop road. For months there had been a car stuck in a ditch that we always passed but this time the creature was perched on top of the car. We drove by so fast that I didn't see what happened to it but it was once again a super clear night with a full moon so I saw it very well. Nobody else saw it because my cousin was asleep and my friend driving was focused on the road. On our ride back the creature was gone."

Original sketch provided by the eyewitness.

Follow up dialogue

NB: It's not often people see these things multiple times.

M: I don't understand it. I'm not sure if it's the same thing I keep encountering or multiple. As soon as I heard about this book I finally felt like I wasn't alone because I haven't heard anyone really talk about it before. I've done some research but I haven't really found anything that made sense.

NB: So many people are reporting very similar encounters but nobody seems to be cataloging these reports and unfortunately there isn't much about it that makes sense.

24

"JAMES JORDAN" (ALIAS) AND OTHERS

NAME OF EYEWITNESS	"James Jordan" (alias) and others.
DATE/TIME OF SIGHTING	Spring, 2019.
LOCATION OF SIGHTING	Shawnee, Kansas.
CIRCUMSTANCES PRIOR TO SIGHTING	Hanging out in a park.
NOTABLE SIGHTING DETAILS	Multiple pairs of illuminated eyes.

Initial statement

"Okay, so my friends and I frequent a park in Shawnee, KS. It's right on the Kansas River and we go there quite often. There have been a couple nights where we've seen small human-like creatures that are a very pale white, have bright yellow eyes, and they tend to stand behind/in trees, swaying their bodies back and forth like an upside-down pendulum.

I've had a couple buddies say that they've seen them too. A couple farmers in the area say they've seen their eyes bobbing back and forth from a distance without needing any source of light to cause them to glow.

The one thing that every story has in common, including my own, is that they can move so fast, that they almost look like lightning shooting across the treeline (one farmer even claiming that he saw one clear a 1/2 mile gap, in the blink of an eye). I've seen them a few times but in all of my experiences, they've stood about 4'9", been incredibly docile and skittish, and generally only appear on foggy nights. Besides the fog, they don't seem to match up to any popular stories I've ever heard about Skinwalkers, Wendigo, or Rakes but the similarities in appearance, besides size, match up perfectly.

<u>Follow up dialogue</u>

JJ: I don't have dates or full names, I would just talk to people in passing. We've been using that park in Shawnee, KS as a hangout spot for around two years now and honestly never really noticed anything strange up until about a year ago.

I was moving out of my roommate's place. Times were tough and I needed a release so we all drove out to the river to party and blow off steam. After a couple hours of us drinking, we started hearing voices down the river so a couple of us started walking along the bank. Finally, I turn to my left and see a bunch of yellow eyes in the distance with one set swaying back and forth slowly. We stay in place. My buddy turns his flashlight on and we realize it's just the reflectors on one of our trucks but the swaying set disappeared. I didn't think much of it, wrote it off as paranoia and went back to partying.

Fast forward to earlier this year in the spring and we go out again. At this point, a guy that I had worked with had warned me about his own experience with those eyes and that they chased him out of the river through the woods. It was at this point that I started asking local farmers if they had seen anything.

A guy by the name of Evan told us about multiple accounts of the eyes. He could see them from about 1/4 mile away and he was in the middle of a 1/2 mile wide clearing. Thought it was a bird but the eyes were bothering him so he fired a round at it. The second he pulled the trigger it vanished. He saw a white flash across the clearing. He turned around and there it was 1/4 mile away clear on the other side of the field. The same night he was telling me this, I saw multiple of them just standing behind trees and rocks, refusing to come close to us.

NB: Did he describe what they looked like?

JJ: I haven't really told anyone about it other than a couple of other people in my family but I think it needs to be out there. Don't know if it truly was a "Crawler" or some other humanoid-type unidentified creature but it was something weird. It's nice to know that people care and actually listen and take it seriously because it was as serious as a heart attack in that moment and it still haunts both my grandpa and me to this day.

NB: Just the eyes?

JJ: And the streak of it moving through the field.

25

NICK BUSH & MARGARET MAGSTADT

NAME OF EYEWITNESS	Nick Bush & Margaret Magstadt
DATE/TIME OF SIGHTING	May 2019 at around 10 p.m.
LOCATION OF SIGHTING	San Francisco Bay Area, California.
CIRCUMSTANCES PRIOR TO SIGHTING	Driving back to Mr. Bush's residence from Ms. Magstadt's.
NOTABLE SIGHTING DETAILS	"Tall, skinny, pale-skinned" subject bent over a deer carcass.

Initial statement

"I live in the San Francisco Bay Area. There is a stretch of road between me and my girlfriend's house that goes through some ranches and a wooded area. My girlfriend and I were driving back towards my house around 10 p.m. While I was rounding a corner near the beginning of the woods, I swerved as I saw what looked like a tall, skinny, pale-skinned person standing by the side of the road and walking into the road. When I looked in my rear mirror to see what it was I couldn't see anything but after I asked my girlfriend about it she was clearly shaken and said she saw it too. We decided to stop talking about it for the time being and continued to drive deeper into the woods back home.

Eyewitness sketch provided by Ms. Magstadt.

About 15 minutes down the road, we came across a fresh deer carcass on the side of the road and while I noticed the deer carcass alone, as I was focusing on the narrow road, my girlfriend swears she saw the same figure bent over the carcass. I drove by that carcass for weeks after when I went back to her house. We've both seen a lot of weird stuff on that small stretch of road, including more on that specific drive, but nothing else that I'd think would have been a Crawler. I'm not sure where it came from (no caves I'm aware of) or if it was more than one out there but I know to always be aware of what else is on that road with me late at night."

26

ANONYMOUS 8

NAME OF EYEWITNESS	Anonymous.
DATE/TIME OF SIGHTING	First: Summer of 2000 or 2001 "after midnight." Second: Spring of 2006, approx. 8 p.m. Third: June 8, 2019, approx. 11 p.m.
LOCATION OF SIGHTING	First: Southern New Hampshire. Second: Central Florida. Third: Eastern Shore of Virginia.
CIRCUMSTANCES PRIOR TO SIGHTING	Varied.
NOTABLE SIGHTING DETAILS	Three different encounters throughout three different states. Extreme emotional toll on eyewitness.

Initial statement

"I saw a thing in, or near, the woods on three separate occasions now. Each time I saw the thing, it was in a different state along the east coast of America and each time the sighting was fleeting. I'm in my 30s now and the sightings have several years between them. The first time I saw it was in high school and this is most definitely the time I got the longest look at it. The second time I only caught a glimpse and I'm pretty sure (but not entirely sure) it was the same thing. The third time I got a clear look at it from a distance but it caught me so off guard that I stumbled as I was taking a step and I lost sight of it.

I have been calling it a thing because I have no idea what it is and quite honestly I don't even have a good guess either. It was not a Sasquatch, a wildman, a Rake, a lizard person, or any other creature I have found through my incredibly frust- rating recent internet research on the subject matter. Maybe a shapeshifter of some kind because the first time I saw it the thing changed its form for sure. Yes, I said it changed its form. You can go ahead and leave now if you like.

If you are someone like me that will rely on science for validation, you try to keep an open mind but you also tend to explain away people's paranormal encounters for any number of different reasons. Also, I would have expected that if I ever did end up seeing some- thing otherworldly, it might be something that someone else had seen before, right? I might see something I recognized from television or movies and I might say, "Look up there! That's a UFO!" or "Holy sh-t, a ghost!" or "G-ddamn, is that a Bigfoot? Kill it!" This thing though ya'll, this f--king thing, it was so surreal and so deranged looking I'm really at a loss.

This post is the first time I have put any of this out there to anyone and if it weren't for this last encounter, I would have forgotten the first two again. I have never mentioned this to anyone because of how ridiculous it sounds. The fact that I have no proof and the fact that I am a known f—k about; I'm pretty much exactly the person you would think might make something like this up. At this point though, I only want to get this off my chest to hopefully find out if anyone else has ever seen this thing.

Before I begin telling you what happened, I would like to make it clear that I swear what you read here is the truth about what I saw as best as I can remember. If you don't believe it, fine, whatever, I get that. This is the reason I am posting what happened here and it is the reason that I have never, and will never, told anyone I might have to see in my daily life. I'm sure they would think I'm crazy or just desperate for attention because what I saw is downright absurd. I have been thinking about exactly how I might explain this to someone for a while now, so I will do my best to keep out of a narrative tone.

Well, now that I have thoroughly destroyed any credibility I may have once had, I will attempt to explain the details about what I saw as bluntly as possible with as vivid of a recollection as I have of the events.

First Sighting: Southern New Hampshire – 2000 or 2001

Summer probably (I don't remember exactly when). Well after midnight.

I am going to take some time to explain this first encounter in as much detail as I can recall even though it all happened so fast, literally lasting in total maybe ten seconds, it is still the longest amount of time I have spent truly looking at the thing. I was walking to a friend's house from the apartment complex I lived in late at night. To get from one place to the other quickly, you had to cut through a small patch of forest (roughly 100 yards) that was technically someone else's property. A couple of times before we had someone shine a light on us and once he fired a shot in the air to try and scare us in an attempt to get us to stop cutting through though, but it never did stop us. It did, however, teach me to be stealthier when cutting through, and so on this night; I was creeping very quietly through the trees as I went. The forest was in a valley between my apartment complex, some houses, and the neighborhood where my friend lived. The valley dipped down in the middle with a steep incline surrounding it and so at first; I had to go down into the valley, and then at the end, I would walk up out of the valley exiting the treeline right onto the street where his house is. Once exiting the tree line, one would be standing on the side of the street with the end of the road about half a mile to your right and the entrance to the neighborhood about the same distance on the left. The houses were spaced apart decently, so the night was very dark except for the area around the houses and a couple of light circles under the orange streetlights, of which there were very few for the amount of space. I got through the valley with no problem this time, and I got up some speed to go up the hill in front of me where the forest ended maybe five feet from the edge of the street if it was even that far. At the exact moment I came out of the treeline and onto the edge of the road; something caught my eye to the left of me emerging from the woods across the street. It stumbled awkwardly out of the dark woods and into view right at the edge of the circle of orange light radiating down from one of the streetlights. At first and for just a brief moment it looked like a shadow; however, I heard a sound coming from the dead leaves beneath its feet, and I quickly realized that it was not a shadow. Its body shape was like that of a starving child (maybe three feet tall) that you might see in a third-world country, but its legs and arms were so thin that there appeared to be no way it could support the creature's body weight.

It was dark but from what I can remember at the ends of its frail-looking limbs were just nubs; no hands and no feet that I saw. Its movements were the creepiest part honestly, and they were the first thing that threw me off. I can't even really explain how absurd and unnatural its movements were or how it was standing on those tiny legs. It moved forward from the trees and toward the street extremely awkwardly with the couple of steps that I saw it take. It was almost as if it was not supposed to be walking around like that, but it had somehow figured out a way to do so regardless. The thing was roughly two or three feet tall with an enlarged light bulb-shaped head and a little belly in spite of how thin the rest of its frame was. In addition to its shape and motion, the thing seemed unreal mostly because it didn't seem to reflect any light at all when it stepped into the light of the street lamp. It appeared to have no three-dimensional form at all with its body almost blending right into its shadow, and I could only really tell it had solid form by the way that it moved and navigated the environment around it. I froze in place instantly when I saw it with my brain unable to even process what I was seeing. In a couple of steps, it exited the trees, stumbled across the patch of grass to the street, and then sort of fumbled down forward toward a sewer drain on the side of the road.

I'm not sure what I did if anything, but as soon as it hit the curb, it rose back up and looked over at me. I couldn't see its face or anything at all, still, just this bizarre black shape moving so unbelievably awkwardly; I really can't stress this enough; its movements were ridiculously uncoordinated. What happened next is what sent me fleeing into the woods with all of the cowardice that has kept me alive to this day. Upon seeing me, this malformed shadow child thing did this quick twisted turn toward me, dropping down to all fours and becoming a much more animal-like shape when it did.

I again have no idea how to describe the motion as it was so unnatural, but when its turn was complete, the thing had become something I can only describe as a shadow dog/cat/bear. I know that sounds crazy but, I can't describe it any other way than that. It stood on all fours like a predatory animal, but I couldn't make out any definition on it with the way it didn't catch the light that it was standing directly below. This thing, it didn't just go from being human-like to being a human on all fours, I mean it genuinely became something else as far as I can tell.

I debated leaving this next part out because it just slices into the credibility of the events even further, but it happened, and so here it goes. As soon as the creature had hit all fours and was no longer humanoid its eyes flashed yellow at me, and it let out a loud shriek, not a growl, not a bark, not a snarl, not an animal-like roar or even a hissing but a legitimate shriek that sounded like neither a person nor an animal. The sound started quietly then rose quickly, almost as if it was winding up or under pressure and had just painfully been forced out of the creature's mouth in great anguish. Its scream had a certain harshness to it as if it might have had something seriously wrong with its vocal cords or it had just smoked a million cigarettes consecutively. I remember the thing had a weird, almost scared vulnerability to the sound it made, which contrasted the harshness and tone as well as the defensive stance the creature took.

All this took place in just a few seconds, maybe ten at most, from the time the thing exited the treeline to the time it turned, postured, shrieked at me, and sent me running without a single thought in my head right back into the woods. I did not stop; I did not look back; I did not try to be quiet through the forest; I just ran as fast as I could. That is correct; I was so scared I ran back into the dark, scary woods to get away, only realizing how dumb that was some time afterward.

The sound it made chilled me to my core then, but now in hindsight, I think the flashing eyes bother me more than the sound because it seems so expected. The flashing/glowing eyes trope is precisely what I have heard in so many other people's stories I never believed about mysterious creatures they claim to have encountered. I mean because that is what scary things in the night do right? They flash yellow eyes and make a scary shrieking sound at you, obviously, what else would they do? I never made it to my friend's house that night, and I never mentioned this to anyone ever since. I managed to forget about this experience pretty quickly although I'm not sure how my life was high-drama at the time, so I'm sure it is because I did something stupid and that took over my world.

Second Sighting: Central Florida – 2006 Spring (I believe) – Early night (8 p.m.)

The second sighting is much briefer and as I mentioned before I am 90% sure it was the same thing but, I'm not entirely sure. I'll keep this short and tell you simply that I was out camping, went for a walk along a trail, and watched my girlfriend hop from rock to rock across the river. I heard a sound to my left, and when I turned to look, I saw an extremely thin skinny black nubbed leg (possibly a tail) disappear behind a tree as if an animal running away from something. I ran over this time but I found nothing and I didn't mention it to my girl-friend. No experiences or weird sounds that night and no more encounters for several years. If you like more detail about this one you can attempt to email me with any questions and I will try to remember.

<u>Third Sighting: Eastern Shore of Virginia</u> – June 8, 2019 – Late night (11 p.m.)

Well finally here it is the reason I felt I had to put this out there and the reason I am so freaked out by this thing. It's not so much what happened last week as it was another quick glimpse and nothing else, but instead, it is the fact that it happened again to me and as far as I know, no one else.

Last week I was at a party at a friend's house celebrating her birthday because she is one of those people in their 30s that still gets excited about those things. I don't drink, so I was not drunk but, in the interest of total transparency, I have been known to partake in the occasional medicinal herbal supplement for recreational purposes. You can take that information however you like. My friend lives with her husband in a farmhouse surrounded by open fields for a couple of acres in any direction surrounded of course by a thick forest. I had been there for a while, and the thing was the furthest thing from my mind. We were all just hanging out and rambling on about the usual inane bullshit. I decided that I wanted a smoke and so I went out the front door and onto the porch. I stepped forward and went to step down the front steps to get a little more space, and as I did, I glanced up and out into the field in front of the house. There it was, roughly 50 yards out and bumbling through the field toward the trees. For a split second, I could see the unmistakable shape of this weird shadow child thing. It was just the same as before; large head and belly, unbelievably thin arms and legs, and again reflecting absolutely no light at all. I was mid-step when I glanced up and lost track of where I was stepping, causing me to fall forward. I managed to catch myself as I fell barely and I must have made a sound when I did it because when I looked back up the thing was on all fours quickly running like a dog off into the woods. I reiterate this thing DID NOT move on all fours like a person in any way but, it moved like an animal with knees bent backward. I was too far, and it happened too fast for me to tell if it had hands and feet this time. I started to walk out and look around a bit when someone came outside and not wanting to tell anyone I just went back to the party. I must have been distant the rest of the night because I couldn't get it out of my head this time. I ended up leaving the party relatively early and went home to start obsessing about it, as I have been, for about a week now.

So I am sufficiently freaked out by a lot of things about what I have seen. Even discounting the second sighting, I got two brief but good looks at something that I can not explain. One of the things that bother me the most about this is, why me? Why, as far as I know, have I been the only one to see this thing? If it knows of me and is following me or something like that then, why does it seem surprised by my presence each time I've seen it and then enter a sort of fight or flight mentality. If it doesn't know of me, then why am I the only one to see this thing and now in three different states years apart? I have so many questions! I'm writing this over a few days to make sure I have got all the details as best as I can remember and I hope I'm not the only one that saw this creepy little f--ker.

What I saw that night was so unnatural I never expected to see anything like it in my life, it honestly just DID NOT belong in our physical reality, and it almost did not even seem to fit in the environment around it as if it was something 2D superimposed into an authentic 3D background. I looked into shadow people videos and sightings but, I don't think this was that as there was nothing ghostly about what I saw, it was there and had solid form. This thing ya'll, this fucking thing, it was so out of place but at the same time I saw it there and heard it as well, I don't know what else to say about it. Each time (except the second) I could see enough of it that I could tell it was not somebody messing with me, and I could see enough of it to say it did not belong here in this world with us. My best guess at this point is that it and I crossed each other's paths in a possible inter-dimensional rift or time slip only because of how surreal the experience was. I know that sounds crazy, but it is all I have come up with to rationalize the fact that this thing did not fit into its surroundings in any way. It did not even look like it was made to move and get around in this world; the force of gravity should have for sure crushed its skinny legs under the weight of its body, it was like an eggplant on toothpicks.

That is all that it is for me to tell, but I sincerely hope someone else saw something like this, so I know I am not starting to lose it. At this point, I only want to know that I am not alone and that what I saw has some explanation, rational or not - I don't even care please, just give me something to go on. I need one reasonable answer from somewhere at this point because I know what I saw, and I can't get the way this thing moved or how dark it was out of my head."

An artist's interpretation based on the eyewitness's description.

Follow up dialogue

"The following is the most challenging thing I have ever had to write and I'm really not sure where to even begin as the events have forced me to confront things about my past that I have tried to bury for a long time. I ask that you please bear with me, this probably isn't what you want to hear, and it is definitely not something I want to say, so much, so I even considered making something up or just never coming back. It is your generous responses to my first post that convinced me otherwise, and so I will now do my best to explain.

After talking to friends and family in order to straighten out some dates I was unclear on, I believe I have found a correlation between all of my encounters. There is no comfortable way to say this, so I'll just say it; in August of last year my pregnant girlfriend had a miscarriage, and this is now the third child I have lost pre-birth.

In my junior year of high school, I got my girlfriend at the time pregnant, and her parents forced her to get an abortion before I was even aware of her pregnancy. We were kept separated, and she broke off contact with me shortly after, I haven't spoken to her since. This occurred a few months after my first encounter with the thing, and the emotional fallout may have contributed to me putting that first encounter out of my head so quickly.

In June of 2006, sometime after my second encounter, my girlfriend at the time was in a car accident when her friend lost control of her car in the rain and hit a telephone pole with my girlfriend riding shotgun. My girlfriend's chest and abdomen hit the dashboard, causing her to break a few ribs, which caused a minor internal laceration. She was taken into surgery, and the surgeons (God bless those people) were able to fix the damage and save her life; however, it was at this point that we learned she was about one month pregnant. Due to the injury from the accident, however, she was unable to bring the baby to term, and a medically induced abortion was necessary. (There is some family controversy about whether or not this was necessary but, I trust the doctors.) If I recall correctly, insurance paid most of the plastic surgery bill for the scar on her chest, and eventually, I paid for a massive tattoo to cover it up at her request. In all honesty, I never cared about the scar but it obviously affected her mentally, and she often over-dramatically referred to herself as "damaged" or "broken," neither of which I ever saw as accurate. I stayed and supported her through the recovery, but this was the beginning of the end of our relationship as she became hooked on painkillers shortly after. I stayed as long as I could, and some people tell me I stayed longer than I should have, but I really cared about the person I knew before the drugs. Soon, however, it became abundantly clear to me that, after a few years of fighting for her, the person I had once known was never coming back. This has eaten at me ever since, and I often wonder if I could have been around more for her but, I was the only one working at the time, and I had to double down on it to support us both. I still have yet to recover totally from the financial hole that this put me in, and as far as I know, she has yet to kick her addiction, we haven't talked in years. Again I believe the trauma and fallout are what made me put the encounter out of my mind, and I never made a connection between the two events.

In July of last year, just shortly after the third encounter, it happened again when a friend and I hooked up on a whim, and she had an abortion just weeks after us discovering her pregnancy. I all but begged her not to, but she was dead set on getting it done immediately because she had a boyfriend that I was previously unaware of at the time, so I just ended up letting it happen. It tore me apart inside, and I had been pretty damn solitary since then, that is until I met the woman that I am currently dating. She is so amazing, and I love her deeply; she is smart, beautiful, thoughtful, and so much more mature than me. She makes me a better man just by being around, and she pulled me out of my self-imposed solitary confinement and then somehow managed to get me feeling like myself again rather quickly. This is where I want it all to end, but, of course, almost immediately after we started dating, that f---ing piece of shit, little thing came back and in the weirdest goddamn way.

I made sure to note as many of the details as I could this time since so many people asked good questions last time that I couldn't answer because I didn't think to remember. I again tried and failed to stay out of a narrative tone, but either way, I think I still did well enough, getting out all the details as factually accurate as possible.

This latest encounter took place on Friday, August 5, 2019, at approximately 7:30 p.m. as I was walking from my Jeep to the duplex I live in after getting back from work. The sun was setting behind me as I pulled into the short driveway in front of my home. The sun had gone down to the point where it was below the treetops yet still not at the horizon, so there was still some ambient light left in the day. It was incredibly hot that day, like pushing 100, and it had only cooled off a little bit by that point, with the humidity still at 100 percent.

My neighborhood is lower-middle-class, so all of the houses are small but there is a bit of space between each of them giving everyone a little elbow room at least. The street I live on is a cut-through between two parts of our small town, so even though we are pretty rural, the road out front actually gets pretty busy sometimes. My place is just a few yards off of the street, and I have a backyard that extends out about twenty feet behind the building before stopping abruptly at the patch of trees dividing my neighbor's lawn from mine. As usual, I parked in the gravel about 20 feet from the edge of the screened-in patio where my girlfriend was sitting on the porch swing. She gets off work much earlier than I do, and she is usually there with a drink in hand each weekday when I got home (None of this seems relevant; I'm just trying to cover anything and everything this time).

I parked on the left side of my house, grabbed my things, got out, and started walking around the front of my Jeep toward the house. As soon as I got out of the vehicle, I began to hear a clicking sound in my ears but I thought it was just sinus pressure or something at first because it sounded like it was inside my ear canal. My girlfriend was on the phone, but she smiled and waved at me as I walked up and it was at that exact moment when I looked up at her, that I saw it out of the corner of my eye. I quickly looked over, and there it was as clear as can be, standing at the edge of the little patch of trees. Per usual, as soon as I saw it, it saw me.

The thing is roughly three feet tall and shaped like a starving child with a possible deformity. It has no discernible features or shape, and it is essentially just a flat black space in the place where its substance and form should be. It's almost as if it was cut out of reality or like the physical space that it occupies/exists in is just totally voided out negative space. I don't know how else to describe it, that's the best I've got.

Something very different that freaked me out about this

encounter happened in that instant we first noticed each other. When the thing turned its "head area" toward me and leaned back off of the tree a bit, I saw its arms were extending maybe 25 or 30 feet straight up the trunk of the tree and into some of the leafier branches at the top. This completely froze me in my tracks for a second even after swearing that I would be ready for it the next time it showed up. Its "arms" were thin and filled with the same empty blackness as before but they (like its movements) just didn't seem to be natural for it. Its arms were almost fluid-like in their motion or slithering like snakes, sort of. It's so tough to explain because the whole thing never does seem to belong in its surroundings at all, but again, the way it moves its body really just doesn't line up with the way it is shaped. I'm still not sure if it's the actual motions of the thing or if it is its lack of any three-dimensional form but, looking at this thing is so disorienting. It's hard to tell what it's doing when it moves, how big it really is, or even how far away it is. I could only be sure of its location this time because I know where the tree is that it was standing against. This all happened in about three seconds, and just like every other time, I have a brief second (or two) where my brain is just unable to process what I'm seeing in front of me even though I've seen it before several times now.

I'm not actually sure if it ran from me the first time as I turned and ran away from it at top speed that time, though it was definitely startled to see me. We were much closer to one another the first time than any other time so, maybe it went fight instead of flight in that instance, I don't know. That's assuming it even thinks and reacts like a rational living creature at all.

It was just so much more creepy this time with those crazy arms, like a demented evil little inflatable tube man, which I'm sure sounds funny until you actually see it. I hadn't gotten a look at this thing so clearly since the first time, and it's been so long since then that the memory of that first encounter has since slowly been fading away. It was roughly the same as before in shape and size but no eyes at all this time that I could see, and yet again, I am struck by how infinitely dark this thing is. (I know this is something that I keep repeating, but

I still don't think I have accurately depicted just how empty the area it fills is.) Every time that I have seen the thing, it has been as if I spotted it doing something that it shouldn't have been doing although, now I don't believe it was as surprised as it seemed to be to see me. If it weren't for the jarring and bizarre sight of its long clumsy "arms," I might have reacted quicker but, I did alright at the time, I guess. Possibly because when I saw it standing there so plainly out in the open, a weird sense of validation for my crazed Reddit post and all the ensuing drama came over me. At that moment, right then, I was so totally sure I was going to get a picture of it or that when I yelled to my girlfriend, she would then turn and see it standing there as well. I didn't react the way I did the previous times for sure because I dropped my tool bags on the ground and went running into the backyard at a full sprint while yelling my girlfriend's name. I guess I didn't seem excited enough when I called out to her because my girl-friend just held up the "wait a minute" finger while slowly and casu-ally standing up off the swing bench to try and see what I was running towards. I reached for my phone but immediately realized that it was in the backpack that I had just dropped, which caused me to briefly freeze and almost go back for it but, then I kind of just double-clutched the decision instead and took off running after it. I honestly thought I had a better chance of getting to it, than getting back to my bag, digging out my phone, and then running over to get a picture. (I legit thought I was going to catch it but, I never got anywhere close in the end. Stupid, I know, get your camera out, you f---ing idiot. Also, in case you are wondering, I have no f---ing clue what I would have done if I had gotten close enough to grab it.) Well, I must have lost sight of it for a split-second during that brief pause because I can't remember how it got into the next position I saw it in but, it had somehow now gone from having its "head" turned toward me and standing on two legs to being down on all fours bounding away from the tree and back into the brush. It happened so fast it was like it didn't turn or move to be facing the other direction, it just all of a sudden was facing the other direction, in a different shape, moving a totally different way. I was about 15 ft. (I'm bad at judging distances) away from it as it ran off and just kind of disappeared behind some bushes, just like when I saw it across the field in front of my friend's house. Also, I'm not sure if I mentioned this, but from this encounter and the previous one, I got the impression that it was more comfortable on all fours.

I didn't/couldn't hear any sound at all coming from the creature via vocalization or interaction with the environment. Possibly, I didn't hear anything this time because of the tapping sound in my ears, or perhaps it's because there is a lot of action in my neighborhood, and it gets a little noisy.

I didn't follow the thing into the woods because simultaneously when I lost sight of it, I also got distracted by the sight of something up in the tree out of the corner of my eye. When I got to the tree, I looked up just in time to see both of the thing's "arms" sliding/slithering back up the tree, moving like a tape measure made of black spaghetti being retracted back into its holster. It looked like it had either detached its arms and ran off without them, or even maybe that there was another one up in the tree that had been reaching down to it, which is precisely what I thought was going on at the time. For a brief moment, I even idiotically felt that I had cornered another one of them (if there are any more) up in the tree and that I might also catch it somehow.

Regardless, at this point, I was now standing at the base of the tree looking way up the trunk where I saw its "hands" (which I haven't seen it have any other time) with slender "fingers" tapping on a high branch making a typing motion as if it had a keyboard up there sitting on the tree limb. It was then that I realized what the sound in my ears was; it was the very distinct sound of typing on a keyboard, although the noise in my ear was not any louder now that I was closer to the tree than it was when I was across the backyard. The noise wasn't loud in general, but it sounded like it was right inside my ear, and it sounded familiar, like the keyboard on my computer inside my home. (Obviously, this last statement may be me overthinking, but, at that moment, I felt like it was a memory of the sound of me typing being replayed in my ear rather than a noise coming from an outside source. If that makes any sense.) It happened so fast again, and after just a second or two, its "arms" slid up behind the bottom of the branch as its "hands" simultaneously stopped typing and pulled down behind the top of the same tree branch where they both disappeared completely. *(The lack of shadow and depth put against something that does reflect light is a difficult thing to explain until you actually see it. It makes it near impossible to tell distances or what direction anything is moving, so it almost looks like its always coming towards you or going away from you.)*As soon as the "arms & hands" were gone entirely, I briefly checked behind me to make sure it wasn't still there and gave a quick look around the trees for the thing making sure to keep aware of the treetop area but, I never saw anything again. I then turned back around and walked around the tree a couple of times, but I saw nothing up in the sparse covering the tree provided. I checked all around and even threw some rocks up there to see if I could get something to move around but, obviously, nothing. The sound in my ears stopped as quickly as it started, and I knew then that the thing was gone.

By this point, my girlfriend had hung up the phone and was standing in the doorway to the porch shouting at me, asking what is going on, and I'm now down in the backyard wondering how the f--k to explain it. When I asked my girlfriend if she "saw that," she responded with those two deflating words; "Saw what?" and it made my heart sink so low because I knew it had just happened again. It was right f---ing there and apparently caught in an awkward position with seemingly nowhere to go. My girlfriend was right there for validation as well, I thought, and yet again, I got nothing. I explained it away as saying that I thought I saw a black bear but, it must have been a raccoon, and my girlfriend shrugged it off quickly enough only after giving me shit for throwing rocks at what I foolishly told her was a raccoon.

Not only is this thing incredibly frustrating with how it continually is able to avoid giving me proof, but the whole scenario just made me feel like an idiot. I feel like it tricked me for some reason but, I don't know why, which in itself is also eating me up inside. I've gotten over trying to piece together the specifics of each event as they are all so similar in some ways but so different in others. The arms, the flashing eyes, turning into a dog-like thing, the sound it made – I mean what the f--k is all that?

It wasn't until a bit later that night that the full extent of what this encounter meant dawned on me. My girlfriend was working on her laptop (graphic designer), and I just kept staring at her. She's so beautiful, even with the cold blue reflection of the computer screen filling her glasses and covering her big brown eyes. I distinctly remember a moment that night when she looked up and caught me staring at her; I smiled at her, and she smiled back and then asked, "What?" and I, of course, said, "Nothing." That moment broke my heart because I knew then, at that moment, that I wouldn't be able to give her what she ultimately wanted in a child or not even that I couldn't but that if I do, it will inevitably be taken away. It is now my opinion that this thing is some kind of bad omen and I am goddamn terrified, I just don't think I can go through all that loss again.

My girlfriend and I are still together, and there has been no talk of babies yet thankfully but, I would be lying if I said I didn't think I was wasting her time every now and again. I know she wants to start a family someday but I'm so scared and not for me but for her as she deserves so much better than what I know is coming. She deserves to know but, I don't even know how to begin to tell her about this as she is extremely skeptical of the paranormal, just as I used to be. It hurts so much to go through losing a child, even one you never got to meet. I love her so much, and I don't want her to feel the kind of pain and suffering that I have felt from the loss. My hands are trembling as I'm typing this, and I can't stop grinding my teeth. I hate this thing. I hate it so f--king much."

27

ANONYMOUS EYEWITNESS AND OTHERS

NAME OF EYEWITNESS	Anonymous eyewitness and others.
DATE/TIME OF SIGHTING	Fall 2017, spring and summer 2019.
LOCATION OF SIGHTING	Wyoming, Michigan.
CIRCUMSTANCES PRIOR TO SIGHTING	Being in or around Resurrection Cemetery.
NOTABLE SIGHTING DETAILS	Multiple sightings between several people.

Initial statement

"I live in Wyoming, Michigan, about a walking distance away from Resurrection Cemetery. If you look it up on Google Maps you will see it has a treeline surrounding it. The treeline closest to the woods is where I've seen it almost every time. I have multiple stories but I'll try to share only the most haunting ones.

The first encounter I had was with my sister. She was going to take a walk through the cemetery. It was late at night (approx. 3:00 a.m.) and I had the gut instinct to go with her, so I did. We decided to play Pokémon GO because why not. I didn't like the forested area around it, especially this big pine tree visible via a maintenance path that led to the crematorium. I was scared out of my mind but we went towards the crematorium anyway to get a PokéStop and a Jigglypuff (a Pokémon). We had to go so close that we were on the maintenance path but the nicer cobblestone half. It was when I looked to my right that I first saw it, hunched over, it looked like a normal human being but more terrifying. It appeared to have seen me too because it stood up, I could tell it was tall, I'd estimate about 7 ft. in height. I told my sister to run and we ran home where I proceeded to pray in my room for a while.

My mom had a sighting as well (approx. 8:00 p.m.). She had mentioned seeing something grey hunched in the top of the pine tree I mentioned earlier watching us. When she looked back it was gone. Safe to say, we went home early that day. I consider myself slightly psychic and when I closed my eyes (sometime around the time that she saw it) I saw two gaping holes staring back at me. My mom described the creature and I recognized it as something I'd drawn a few weeks before. I burned this image but have since redrawn it.

My most recent sighting (and the one that kept me from going back to the cemetery) happened in broad daylight (approx. 4:00 p.m.) with a friend. I'll keep his name hidden for privacy, but we decided to go to said cemetery after class(college program but for high school freshmen). We wandered around the cemetery for hours, until my arm started hurting and I decided that we should go home for a snack. As we walked my anxiety heightened, I had told him about the Crawler but I suspected we wouldn't have to worry as it was daytime. As we were walking along the sidewalk, about to reach the treeline, I saw a dead squirrel/dog arm in the middle of the sidewalk. I looked up and I saw the Crawler run straight into the treeline. It was grey and ran on all fours rather than on two legs. I told my friend to run and he did. We both ran until we reached the intersection."

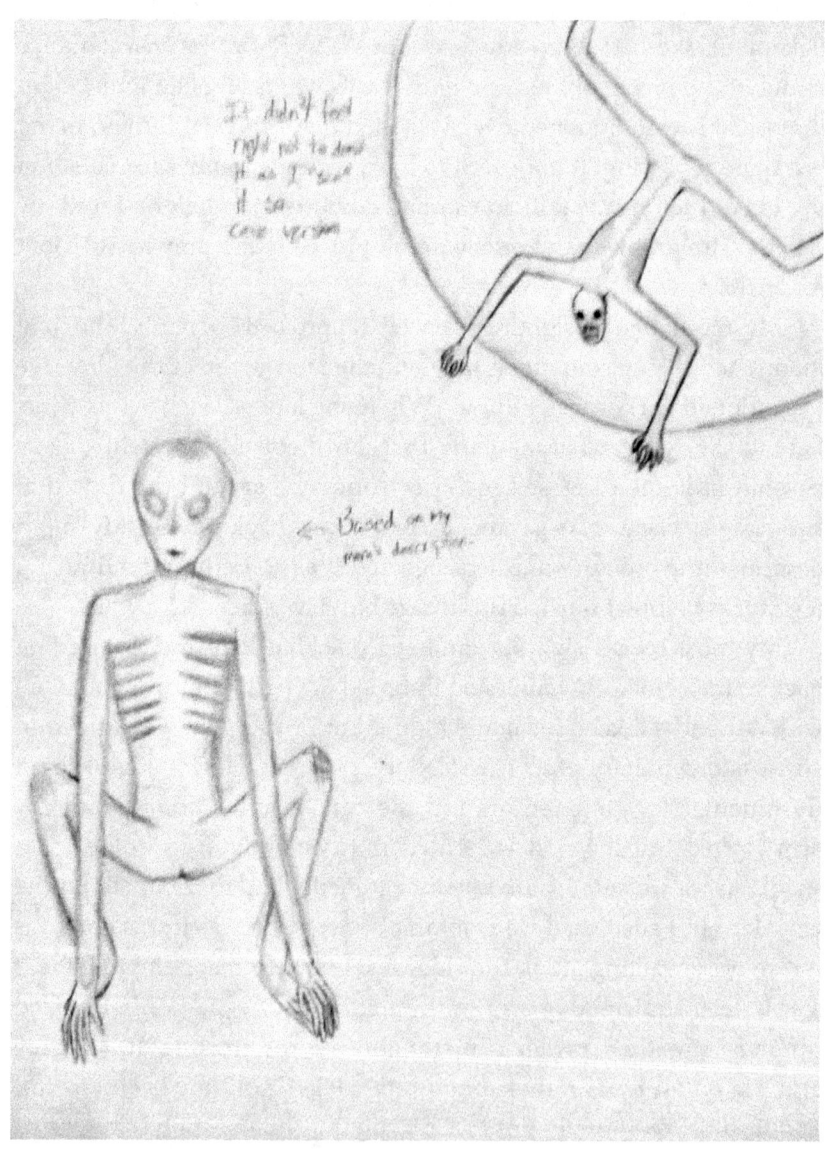

Original sketch provided by the eyewitness.

Follow up dialogue

"The creature was lanky, its arms went almost to its knees. The eyes were sunken in and its mouth looked larger than a normal human's. It was about seven feet in height. (I failed to mention this in my original story but it did growl at me before me and my sister left) It could move really fast as when my mom looked back to confirm what she saw, it was gone. She saw it around 6 p.m. (estimating because I wasn't paying attention to the time). As for the sketches, my mom said she didn't have the time and I'm trying to make a decent picture that isn't in a cave but that's how I always imagine it."

28

ALEX B.

NAME OF EYEWITNESS	Alex B.
DATE/TIME OF SIGHTING	November 6th, 2019 at approximately 11:08 p.m.
LOCATION OF SIGHTING	Granville county, North Carolina.
CIRCUMSTANCES PRIOR TO SIGHTING	
NOTABLE SIGHTING DETAILS	Creature had a pointed head and ears.

Initial statement

"It's currently midnight. This all went down about 45 minutes ago. My brother decided to make a late-night run to the grocery store but on his way back his tire exploded so he called my dad to come pick him up from the gas station he managed to pull into. There are some sketchy folks around that area so my dad suggested we just change the tire and escort him home to make sure the donut didn't go flat too because it's a fairly old spare. My dad calls me and asks me to bring my tools and a jack so we can change the tire. After the donut is on, my dad goes in front and my brother follows, and I follow behind my brother.

We live on a back road off of a back road, with not many houses, lots of farmland, not much traffic, and lots of deer at night. My dad and I turned on the LEDs that we use when we go off-roading when we got to our road so we could see deer well before they were a hazard. The fields stretch about a quarter mile from the road on either side and the lights are bright enough so that I can just barely see the tree line past the fields. We get up to a bend in the road where a small patch of woods separates the field from the house beside it and I see glowing eyes to my left about 15 feet away from the patch of woods on the field side. There were lots of deer out so I was on high alert. I slowed down and kept an eye on it.

The thing had arms, a humanoid shape, and a humanoid head. It was not far from the road, so it was lit up pretty bright and I have no doubts in my mind about what I saw. I was going about 15 miles an hour, it wasn't just a quick glimpse. I looked at it for at least 30 seconds before it was out of view. Once I realized that I had never seen anything like what I was seeing, I started honking my horn and pointing so that my brother and dad in front of me would look but by then they had already passed the patch of woods and couldn't see it. I would guess it was around 6 - 7 ft. tall when standing but it appeared to be either hunched over or kneeling on the ground. It was resting one elbow on something and the other arm was straight. I'm not sure if any of you are familiar with Nosferatu but its head and face looked very similar to Nosferatu's.

It looked gaunt and pale and had pointed ears, and glowing eyes. I am sure the glow was because of the lumens I was shining at it but that at least tells me it's nocturnal. I live in North Carolina if that helps in figuring out what the f--k this is. I'm very concerned because it wasn't far from my home and I've been hearing very strange noises at night for the past few weeks. I took my puppy out to use the bathroom yesterday around 10 p.m. and I could hear something in the forest walking very slow. I know it wasn't a deer because the puppy was barking and it didn't run off. I didn't have a flashlight so I just kept my gun out in case it was a predator and it tried to eat my puppy. It was snapping big sticks, and it sounded heavy. I'm convinced it wasn't a bear because we don't live in bear country. We've never seen bears around here and we go into the woods a lot. We also have a chain link fence all the way around our property line, including in the woods. We inspect it often and I walked the perimeter today and none of it was damaged. Whatever this is, it's agile and smart enough to climb/jump over a fence without noticeably damaging it. A few months ago I also noticed a lot of scratches on the trees around my house, they were all no less than 7 feet off of the ground so in my mind that took mountain lion out of the equation."

Eyewitness sketch provided by Mr. B.

29

MACY REESE

NAME OF EYEWITNESS	Macy Reese
DATE/TIME OF SIGHTING	First encounter occurred in Feb. of 2019 at approx 10 p.m.
LOCATION OF SIGHTING	Mt. Pilchuck State Park, Granite, Washington.
CIRCUMSTANCES PRIOR TO SIGHTING	
NOTABLE SIGHTING DETAILS	"Pinkish pale" skin and "hollow eyes."

Initial statement

"I want to be completely transparent: I'm a fairly sober person. I rarely drink. I do in fact currently eat medical marijuana and CBD for my chronic illnesses (i.e: my PTSD, chronic pain, etc.) I'm seriously certain I know the difference between a bad high versus real life, though to be frank I was sober for each encounter.

I live in the PNW, about an hour or so away from Seattle, in the mountains up in a small logging/mining town that has a large handful of quarries, abandoned mines, caves, and small old abandoned towns in the mountains. My neighborhood is tucked away in the woods with a river running right through most people's backyards.

My first encounter with this creature was, I believe, in February 2019. Sometime around 10 p.m. I was walking my dog up the thin curvy stretch of road that is my neighborhood listening to my typical edgy girl playlist while slowly picking up the speed into a jog. My dog and I continued following the paved road.

Around one of the sharp turns, not even half a mile into my walk, my dog significantly slowed down. His body language changed drastically, he didn't want to go any further. His was focused on a dark patch of pine and maple trees growing on one of the larger fenced-off properties in the neighborhood. I tried to look in the general direction he was staring in and scan the area. I looked past the metal fence sitting in the shadows and I gazed upon a small patch of forest with a creek and a decent-sized pond. My focus was quickly interrupted by an eerily human-like figure standing under the trees in front of the fence. An overwhelming amount of dread quickly washed over me. It felt like all the hairs on the back of my neck were standing straight up... Everything felt wrong. I felt like I was in a horror movie. All I remember was making a run for it with my dog shortly after and not looking back. The empty hollows that we're its eyes still give me the feeling of dread as I type this.

What I saw was not a bear, wolf, coyote, or mountain lion, and it sure as hell wasn't human! Whatever the hell it was it stood on all fours, its elbows were poking out, its ribs were protruding, it had long boney fingers, its spine was poking out a sickening amount, its skin was a sickly pinkish pale, it had no ears and little hair, it had a face but I could barely make anything out. I do clearly remember its hollow eyes.

My second encounter with this creature was only a few months later. I was going on another walk, this time without my dog. It had been a while since I was comfortable going outside at night. This time, in fact, I had gotten a bit further up the neighborhood than the last time. I started walking around the corner just up the hill where I had seen the creature for the first time. I heard a woman scream and it stopped me dead in my tracks.

It sounded off. I don't know how else to explain. I got the weird feeling of dread again. The screams were then shortly followed by nonstop crying. It sounded like it was coming from the forest right off the road. I tried to focus on my breathing and not freak out but I was definitely panicking. I started running up the hill, the crying sounds slowly fading away as I got further. I was panicking. I didn't quite know what to do. I had to run back in the opposite direction for about 1/4 of a mile to get home.

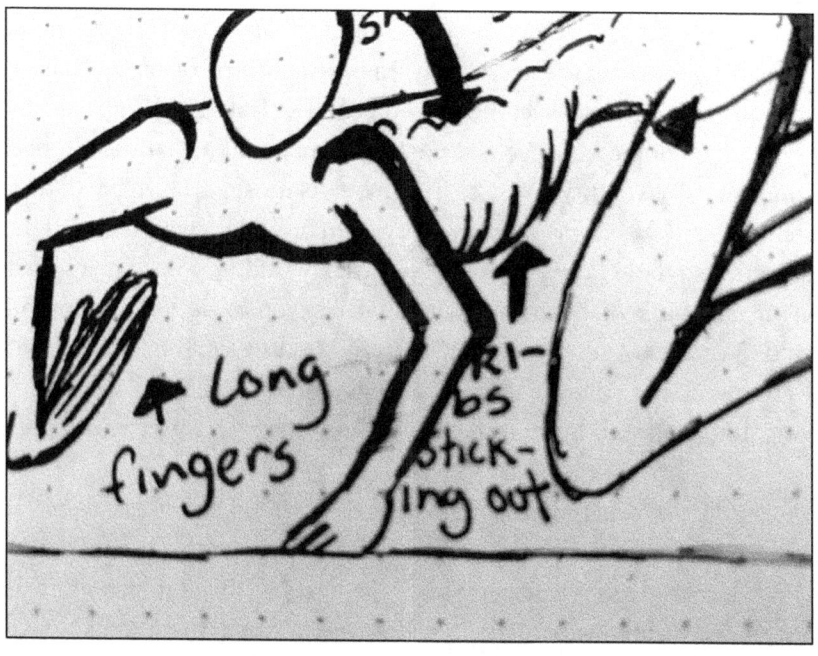

Eyewitness sketch provided by Ms. Reese.

After a few seconds of reassuring myself, I turned around and made a run for it. The crying had completely stopped by the time I had gotten back to where I originally heard it. I didn't care anymore. I kept on running even when I noticed something quickly following me from tree to tree. I didn't see it but I heard something large moving around in the trees after me. To be frank, my stamina is pretty garbage so by the time I needed to take a moment to breathe I was right back where I was when I first saw the creature. I didn't stop for very long because I felt like it was still following me. By the time I was running again, it sounded like something was right behind me. I heard footsteps behind me but I couldn't muster the courage to turn around. Anyway, I'm sorry this story was so long and I was rambling."

Follow up dialogue

NB: Would you be able to describe what you saw in more detail?

MR: I only saw the creature in my first encounter. When it was chasing me in the trees I couldn't see it. It was about 6 - 7 ft. tall, though when I saw the creature it was either sitting or on all fours. I couldn't quite tell so it could have been a little taller. Its spine was protruding out of its back almost in a snake-like manner. It had smallish back empty eyes, slits, where its nose, would be (like a reptile), and it was very, very, very thin. Its skin was really tight around its whole body. It looked very sickly and its skin was a weird veiny pale pinkish, purple off-white. I can't even begin to describe the color. I could not see a mouth of any kind on its face. It had arms that were about the same length as its legs except its fingers were very long. It looked very human-like besides its other inhuman features.

- Also to clarify, in the first encounter when I first heard the woman cry/scream was when I started to run (Note: the scream was not coming from the trees).
- In the first encounter, after I started to run in the wrong direction (which I did because I kept trying to convince myself it was just leaves falling or something but I started to have a panic attack and eventually turned around because of how unsafe I felt) I heard it quickly jumping tree to tree. It was so fast, for the majority of the time I was running from the creature, It was almost always a tree ahead of me.

- In the second encounter I did stop at the same spot I saw the creature in the first encounter (I think it's the same creature.)
- In the second encounter, after I took a few seconds breather and started to run again, that's when I noticed I couldn't hear it in the trees anymore and I heard footsteps behind me.

30

RILEY C.

NAME OF EYEWITNESS	Riley C.
DATE/TIME OF SIGHTING	February 17th, 2020. Approx. 8 p.m.
LOCATION OF SIGHTING	Northeast Georgia.
CIRCUMSTANCES PRIOR TO SIGHTING	Outside with family.
NOTABLE SIGHTING DETAILS	Possible unknown light source above sighted creature.

Initial statement

"To give some context of location, I live in northeast Georgia and at the time this occurred I was visiting some relatives that live in a more rural city than me. To be brief, they live next to a lot of farms.

It was around 8 p.m. when it happened. I walked outside to try and talk to my mom, who was outside with my grandma looking for her glasses, about something I can't remember at the moment.

I walked down the ramp that my relatives built onto their porch and for some reason I felt the need to look into the dark. There were some streetlights here and there but otherwise, it was pitch black.

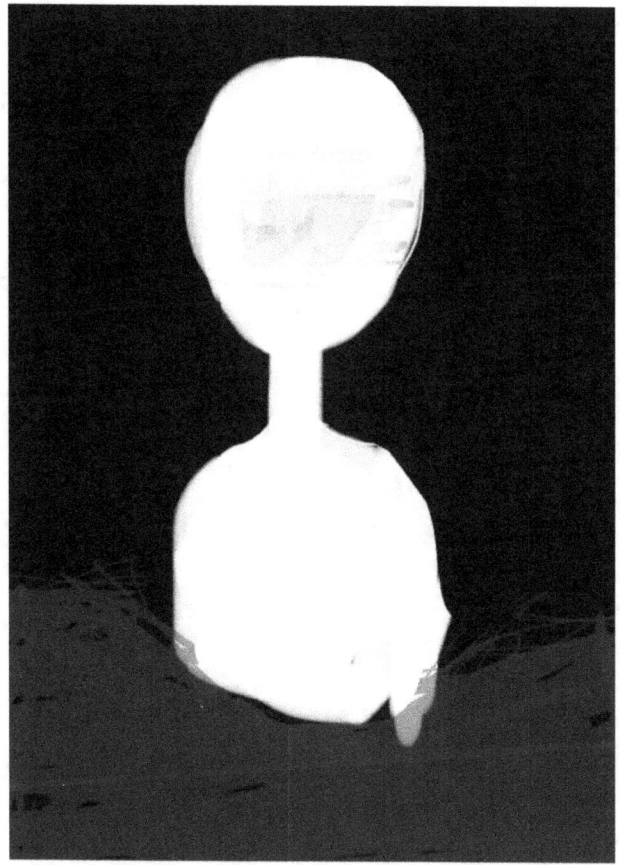

*Eyewitness sketch provided by Riley. Created about 25 minutes
after the sighting.*

Then I saw it. It was standing behind one of my uncle's red tractors and just... staring in my direction. I mean, I didn't see its face
since I have pretty bad eyesight but I know it had one. It was pure
white or maybe light gray. I couldn't tell because it looked like there
was a light directly above it.

All that I could see of it was its upper chest, shoulders, and head
which seemed too big for its relatively skinny neck. I didn't see any
super notable features, sadly. It looked almost like one of those white
mannequins you see in the mall or something except with a big
slightly upside-down egg-shaped head. As soon as I looked at it, I

noticed that I was starting to shake and my heart was racing as if I just ran a marathon. Of course, I bolted back into the house.

I know it wasn't just my eyes playing tricks, because when I went out there about 15 minutes later, it was gone. I was too scared to go out there alone again after running back inside."

31

ANONYMOUS 9

NAME OF EYEWITNESS	Anonymous.
DATE/TIME OF SIGHTING	March of 2020 at approx. p.m.
LOCATION OF SIGHTING	Western PA, south of Pittsburgh.
CIRCUMSTANCES PRIOR TO SIGHTING	Camping trip. Substance use involved.
NOTABLE SIGHTING DETAILS	Stalking behavior throughout. Mimicking voices in the woods.

Initial statement

"At the time of writing this I am living in western Pennsylvania, a little south of Pittsburgh. I was in Boy Scouts for most of my life so I feel very comfortable in the woods and go camping often. Upon hearing Governor Wolf's school closure plan, I decided that it was time for some cold-weather camping. It was March. It wasn't that cold but it did drop to 40°F at night and the people who I went with weren't really avid campers.

If you're from Pittsburgh you may know the Boggs campsite on the Montour Trail; that's where we went. They, of course, only brought weed and alcohol and didn't bring any sleeping bags, blankets, or pillows so naturally, I assumed they were gonna have to sit by the fire all night.

It was light when we first got there and the fire pit was still smoldering, very cool. We used the coals from the previous camper's fire to light ours and immediately I knew that I would have to provide wood for the fire until I went to bed. They passed out beers at around 3 p.m. (times are gonna be a bit dodgy because I wasn't near my phone) and after having two or three beers I just wanted dinner. Now, that they did for me. They made ramen noodles and cheese which was amazing (they had a weird name for it) and burgers over the fire. By this time it would have had to have been close to 5 p.m. because it started to rain a little bit, as was forecasted, so we took shelter in the lean-to shelter that was on site and occasionally one of them would throw some sticks on the fire (sticks were all they seemed to be able to find even though I brought two saws and an axe) and I would cut up some logs.

By the time the rain stopped, all four of us smoked a blunt and were sitting around the fire. It was still light out so we'll call it 7 p.m. After a while of just hanging out, they asked if I had any blankets. I always have blankets. Nothing special but we've had some pretty bad snowstorms in the past and a couple scratchy car blankets are always useful. They each got a blanket except for R, as we'll call him, who got my summer sleeping bag that I brought just in case. By now it was dark (9 - 9:30 p.m.?) and the fire was getting low. I started off to find some more wood because they wanted to smoke another blunt.

Now you have to understand that I'm 6'5" and a semi-frequent user of the devil's lettuce so my tolerance is kinda high. I return with the wood and we spark up another blunt, a smaller one, and just kinda hang out and talk and listen to music while we're high as sh-t. Good times.

Eventually the fire, again, dies down a little bit and, again, it's my job to get more wood. Because we had been there for a while and there were people there before us, most of the wood near the shelter was either really small or all used up so I had to keep going farther and farther away from camp to find wood.

12:30 a.m. Close to 50°F still so we're all doing well. I had a flash-light, a really nice one that I use for scuba diving, that is kinda bright so I used it on the low setting on land. At this point, I'm far enough away from camp that my friends can't really see me. There's like an embankment between the Montour Trail and someone's driveway that you have to cross to get to more woods but I'm comfortable alone because I knew what I was doing and they could hear me if I needed them.

I started to hear a weird whistling sound, kinda like someone inhaling through a snorkel, but I chalked it up to the wind. The air was starting to get kinda cold so I just took back what I had and put some on the fire.

1 - 2 a.m. ~40°F with some wind, nothing severe. I have on two long sleeve shirts and an army surplus coat that is super warm but my friends are in windbreakers and hoodies and, oh yeah, it's raining. Off to get more wood. This time I started taking into consideration the type of wood that I would collect. There was a lot of pine but that burns fast which is why I had to go collect it so often. The stretch of woods near the driveway was pretty much all pine, with a few maples but nothing big. I kept walking knowing that this area has both conifers and deciduous trees in close proximity to each other.

As I'm wandering and collecting wood I notice that the rain has turned to a super fine snow; time to head back, just in case it picks up. Then the whistling started again, a lot louder now. Okay, weird. There isn't any more wind than there was before. Maybe it changed direc-tions. I kept walking. By now I can hear the music from camp and pick up the pace a little bit. Just as I summit the embankment and prepare to clamber down the other side a loud noise echoes behind me. Tree fell? Shining my flashlight around I couldn't see any signs that this was the case and didn't see any source. Deer knocked some-thing over? In my head, it doesn't matter because I'm back at camp anyways and I can try the marsh behind our shelter next time.

3 a.m.? They were COLD. The temperature dropped to around 30°F and the wind and snow had picked up. Car blankets helped the boys a little bit but they weren't able to go sleep in the tent that I

brought without freezing, except for R who slept like a rock all night after about 3:30. We decided to finish off the weed and give the last beers a good talking to.

4:30 a.m. I'm about ready for bed at this point because I'm not super high or drunk or anything but I was definitely tired. I offer to go collect more wood before I retire to my 0° sleeping bag and cot (I camp comfy when I don't have to carry it far) and they said they would join me. They must have been cold.

We split up and I ended up heading back to where I was before except this time I left my flashlight on high and I made a bunch of noise to scare off that deer or whatever that was there earlier. I ended up a little further away from camp than I had intended to be because there were only pine branches on the ground over here. Then the whistling starts again. This time I could tell the direction it was coming from, my left, and shined my flashlight around that area before just returning to collecting wood.

Then the sound stops briefly before it picks up again in a different direction less than a minute later, this time in front of me and a little to the right, back into the pines. Maybe the branches of certain trees catch the wind just right and make the noise, I thought "whatever" and moved on. Then on my way back, the noise was following me, darting from left to right but always like right behind me. I didn't see anything so whatever. Then the noise made like one sharp whistle and pauses. Then I heard it:

"Damn it's cold out here." It was R but I couldn't find him with my flashlight so I called,

"Where you at?" and it sounded like he turned around because I heard a branch snap and a bit of movement.

I pointed my flashlight at where the sound was coming from and I didn't see R anywhere. Maybe he's behind a bush or a tree or something.

I call out again, "R?"

No reply this time. Yikes. He might be lost or something because we weren't at camp and he saw my flashlight moving so he came to look.

"R, where are you?" Nothing. Then louder,

"I'm going back to camp," because I thought he was trying to scare me.

Shining my flashlight around one last time I spotted something dive into a bush about 40 ft. from where I had heard R turn around.

"I see you, big man. Grab some wood and come back." He's 6 ft. and 230 - 250 lbs. I shine the light around for a few more seconds then turn around again and start walking. The whistling is back. Cool, love that. No matter what speed I moved at, it always seemed the same distance away. I decided that I'd just kinda sit under a tree and wait for R to pass by because he had to come back sometime, right? I wanted to save the battery of my flashlight so I turned it off and closed one eye so it would adjust faster.

By now the snow had picked up a good bit which is another reason to stop in case R got lost. I couldn't really see super far because there was a lot of cloud cover despite it being a full moon. The whistling never got closer but it did start to move around a little bit, in a really odd circle. It would start in one spot, stop, then promptly start in another spot that was in a different direction. I realized that it had to be the wind or something because it was moving super fast and was moving at random. Cool, now where the f--k is R?

I turn on my flashlight between whistles and call out again,

"R?" It's important to note here that the whistling never picked up while I looked around. It normally only stopped for a second or two. It was SUPER quiet. The snow was laying on the ground and we had 2 - 3 in. on the ground by now so maybe that muffled it. Anyways, upon not hearing R I thought that maybe I missed him or didn't hear him at all and started to head back to camp. As I stood up and brushed the dirt off my ass I shined the flashlight around one more time I was thinking in my head, "I definitely heard him." After I stood up with the wood in my arms and began to walk back toward camp I saw something move out of the corner of my eye. My flashlight, being a diving light, has a wrist mount that I was wearing so I could use it and carry things. I turned towards it and scanned the area with my flashlight. Nothing. F--kin' deer. Not even four steps more and I saw more movement and now the whistling was back. Damn, that gets annoying, sounds like a fat guy who just ran up the stairs.

Flashlight was on low so I could see maybe 40 ft. around me and didn't see anything but I knew it was time to pick up the pace. Now the whistling was followed by flashes of movement. Great, it's not the wind. At this point, I'm speedwalking. Being tall I can MOVE if I have to and I was definitely traveling at jogging speed. R, a lumbering beast when he runs, could not move this fast or this quietly through the woods. Nice, another thing that it's not.

I decided to turn off the flashlight and move into some brush that was close by. Not sure why but I was getting a little weirded out and had the shakes even though I was warm. It was silent again. Well f--k me, what is it? Is it hunting me? Coyote? Not a coyote. There was a good period of silence then there was whistling. This time it wasn't doing circles around me. It was just moving around where I had turned off the flashlight. My eyes adjusted and I peeked out from under the bush that I was rolled up under. I tried. Nothing, just that damned whistling.

By this point, I was pretty much sober like if I got pulled over I could NAIL the field sobriety test. I waited for a little while the thing just kinda looked around. Then I heard it speak. In a really gargled impression of me, it called out, "Big man."

It took everything I had not to panic. Holy sh-t. Not R, not human, not a deer, not the wind. Oh, f--k. Then it spoke again, "R," cutting off really strangely like you just lifted the needle off of a record but picking back up again with,

"Back to camp," still in my voice. MY F--KING VOICE. I normally don't like hearing recordings of myself anyways but now I REALLY don't like them. It said a few more things, in different voices that I didn't recognize. All the voices were either talking about how cold it was or questions like "What was that" and "Stop f--king with me" but they all seemed like whoever was talking had some phlegm built up in their throat.

Then it went quiet. I poked my head out of the bushes again and saw something sitting against a tree in the same position I had been in left leg straight out, right leg at an angle, hands behind my head. it could have fooled me as being R. We both kinda sit the same way except his ADHD usually makes him fidget with his hands. So who's sitting in the woods with me?

I lay there, silent, and just watched. It begins to whistle. So that's where that was coming from. It moved its hand around in a fist out in front of it, the same way that I looked around with my flashlight, and then started to stand up. Oh, f--k, it's tall. I only weigh 166, skin and bone mostly, so when I say that this thing was skinny don't take it lightly. I could see how thin its long spindly arms were silhouetted against the snow that coated a bush behind it. When it stood up it was hunched over, not sure if I was slouching when I stood up but I certainly do slouch. It walked a few paces away from the tree and stood up the whole way. HOLY S--T. I worked with backdrops for theater productions and the walls we use the most are around 8 ft. high and this thing would have easily been able to see over one, I'm talking by at least a foot.

It slowly peered around, no hair on its head and its side profile showed a SUPER disfigured skull. The jaw hung pretty far down and there weren't really lips that stuck out but it was hard to tell because of how dark it was. It let out one final,

"R? Big man," kinda like someone with tortures would say it because they were just random words that it strung together. Then it SCREAMED. My dad used to take me to airshows a lot as a kid and this has to have been the same pitch and volume as an F-16.

I couldn't move. It peered around, head just seemingly sweeping the area. Then it crouched down and leaped for a tree with the lowest branch being around 10 - 15 ft. and landed feet first on one of the branches and sits there, squatting, whistling, and just staring around. Then it takes off. Faster than should be allowed in nature. I count to ten in my head. The forest sleeps. I slowly make my way out from under the bush and begin to creep back towards camp, this time avoiding using my flashlight or making any noise if possible. I climb the embankment and take one last look towards the woods, unsure if that just happened or if I was asleep. I tumble down the other side of the embankment and return to the relative safety of the big-ass fire with Y and J, the other two who went for wood.

"Where's your wood?" asks Y.

"Oh it, uh, had bugs."

"It's fine we got a lot anyways." They stacked up a solid pile of oak and pine, not enough for the night but enough for a little while at least.

"Where's R?" I ask warily.

"Check the tent." There he was passed the f--k out, snoring the way he always does. Well, okay then. I climbed into my sleeping bag to warm up a little bit because I was covered in snow when I got back and it screamed again. Oh please don't tell me it's coming here. The other two looked at me wide-eyed. Normally if I recognize a sound I'd say what it is out loud so they know what's up. I had no response. They asked if I heard the first one. Good, they heard it too. I answered with a nod as I unlocked the car in case we needed to book it. They asked if I saw it. Nod. What was it? No f--king clue. I described it to them quietly so that I could listen for more noises and I told them about it imitating my voice. Y was pretty freaked out. J thought I was bullsh---ing him and said it was some kind of owl.

I got out of my sleeping bag, threw my coat back on, and joined them at the fire. For the first time in a while, I looked at my phone. 5:45 a.m. We looked up native owl calls and came up empty-handed. The same happened with every other animal we tried.

J seemed a little nervous. Y suggested that,

"Maybe it's a truck on the highway."

"Yeah that's probably it," I replied blankly and J gave me a look that said that he knew it probably wasn't. They didn't sleep. I forced sleep upon myself so that we wouldn't die on the car ride home.

The next morning we went for a walk. It didn't snow much after I got back so you could kinda follow my footprints. The tree the thing lept into was out of reach from me on J's shoulders. R was still asleep but I think I might have been able to reach it if I was on his.

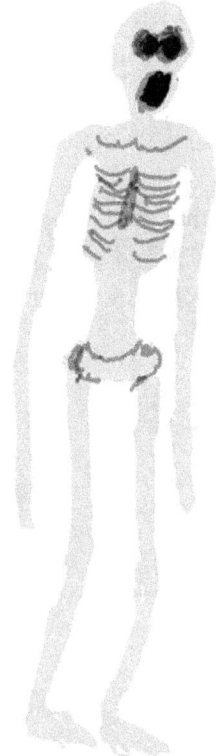

Original sketch provided by the eyewitness.

The tree I sat under had scratch marks on it. I think they're from deer shedding the velvet off of their antlers but it creeped me out nonetheless. The tree it sat under had footprints EVERYWHERE. There seemed to be no order to them at all. It was amazing. It looked like it had run over every square inch of that area, coming as close to the bush I was in as two me-lengths.

I don't really know much about cryptids or anything but when I got home I googled "North American Tall Skinny Cryptid" and the second result was from Parade, a list of cryptids. After ruling out everything else on the list I came across the picture of a Wendigo that has antlers. Not quite but pretty close; described as tall and skinny and super fast. I did my research and every picture has antlers but I can't find any evidence that, other than a few movies, it had antlers.

I don't know. What I saw definitely didn't have antlers but it matched everything else, even down to the whistling."

NB: Do you remember what the footprints looked like?

A: Barefoot and human-ish but they were big and skinny. They looked human but the toes were spread out like a foot high five.

NB: It had five toes?

A: Yes.

32

SHANE KIRBY

NAME OF EYEWITNESS	Shane Kirby
DATE/TIME OF SIGHTING	Late April 2020 at approx. 11:30 p.m.
LOCATION OF SIGHTING	Central Virginia.
CIRCUMSTANCES PRIOR TO SIGHTING	Wandering down forest trails.
NOTABLE SIGHTING DETAILS	A trackway was left by the creature.

Initial statement

"To start off, I live on the east coast in central Virginia and the property I live on contains ten acres of fields and woods. Just as some background info, the property was once a battleground during the Civil War; the Battle of Matadequin took place right around where I live. My friends and I have always seen ghosts and paranormal activity around the property whenever we hang out or camp but that isn't why I'm typing this.

I should probably mention that our campsite contains tarp roofs with pallets set up as walls. I should also mention that we always carry firearms with us in the woods but I'm always enforceable about making sure nobody has any bullets chambered in their weapons unless they have a reason to shoot.

Eyewitness sketch provided by Mr. Kirby.

One night in late April, three friends and I were hanging out by the fire within our campsite. At about 11:30 p.m. one of my buddies and I wandered down the trail with no flashlights of any sort in the dark. We stopped at an opening by the field where we could see the stars. We chatted about random topics for about 5-10 minutes until we started hearing steps and twigs snapping in multiple areas in front of us. We are skeptical but keep an ear out.

All of the sudden, I yelled "Oh, sh-t," and uncharacteristically racked a bullet in the chamber of my rifle as quick as I could. I immediately aimed my rifle toward what I'm seeing. It was dark so I couldn't distinguish the details but this is what I saw... It was a pale white silhouette, it was crawling uphill from another trail. It didn't seem intimidating though, rather intently curious. Its body moved similar to how a chicken bobs its head but more subtle. My friend and I yelled for our other two friends to come assist us.

As the creature got closer, we yelled louder. We weren't terrified, simply frightened and in awe. The creature went behind a tree and repeatedly poked its head out and back behind the tree. It occasionally began to crawl towards us from behind the tree but would retreat once again. All its movements were slow and agile. After about two minutes, it disappeared, as in we couldn't see it because of the brush but it probably fled into the woods.

Our other two friends arrived a minute or so after the creature had fled. Their excuse was that they thought we had run into a hunter or somebody so they decided to take the bullets out of their weapons. Anyway, the next day we went back to the spot of the sighting.

We found disturbed leaves and tracks exactly where we saw the creature. The friend I was with during the sighting is a skilled hunter and tracker. We followed tracks that led towards off the property until it seemed to either go cold or we lost them. We did find a small-sized goat skull in the woods with no carcass to follow near the sighting area."

<u>Follow up dialogue</u>

<u>NB</u>: What did the tracks look like?

<u>SK</u>: I don't think I'd be able to sketch them out very well. Along with an obvious disruption in the otherwise smooth, leaf-covered floor, there were almost holes in the leaves. Imagine digging your heel into leaves in the woods, they looked like that.

33

ANONYMOUS EYEWITNESS

NAME OF EYEWITNESS	Anonymous eyewitness.
DATE/TIME OF SIGHTING	August 14th, 2020.
LOCATION OF SIGHTING	Outside of Charleston, South Carolina.
CIRCUMSTANCES PRIOR TO SIGHTING	In the middle of a walk.
NOTABLE SIGHTING DETAILS	Monkey-like cackling.

Initial statement

"I seriously need help and am terrified out of my mind. So I'll start off by saying I've never believed in anything paranormal. I'm a pretty science-based dude. I always look for a logical explanation, and I still am for this encounter. So if anyone has any ideas let me know.

I don't have much time for leisure with work recently. Been having to accept some pretty awful shifts to get by with COVID times. So, I've lost my ability to go on my evening walks which are a method of stress relief for me. It had been a while since I had gone on one so three nights ago I decided to just go for a late-night walk. I put on my headband flashlight and decided to take a path I hadn't in ages. There's a small trail near the back of my neighborhood that goes about four miles deep into the woods. My plan was to walk about 1.5 miles in and take the parallel path to come back.

I make it down to around 1.3 miles (according to my Fitbit) and I start getting that feeling I'm being watched. I turn off my headlight and sit still to listen. At this point I'm more concerned there's a guy following me who is up to no good. I heard clear footsteps in the leaves off the trail and they'd been behind me for nearly five minutes. I stopped thinking it was an animal or another walker and became worried. Sitting there for probably 3 - 4 minutes and I hear nothing at all. I turn back on my headlight and decide to start walking quickly back home.

About two minutes later I hear footsteps again. This time it sounds different. Sounds like four feet instead of two feet walking. And it's walking at the same Increased speed I am. I turn around quickly with my headlight and my phone light and point them behind me. Silence. I get angry and yell out, "Leave me alone. I'm going to call the cops, and if you come at me I have a knife!" Silence. I yell again [for them] to "get the f--k out of here" and start walking towards where I heard the walking. About 20 yards out (hard to fully make out because the flashlight doesn't reach too far) I see what looks like a literal naked man running full speed on all fours into the woods. Normally I'd chalk that up to drugs but my area does not have a drug problem and there were some details that led me to believe it wasn't a person.

For one, they were damn near hairless; completely bald, with pale white skin, and the way it ran on fours looked natural, not like when you try to run on all fours and look stupid. It looked like its bone structure was designed to walk on all fours. There was no hunched look, their back was flat and they were FAST.

The last thing that happened was straight out of a horror movie. I hadn't heard anything in a while on my way back but kept turning around to be sure. With about .3 miles left to go until I was in the clear, I heard a mad dash through the leaves. I whip around and it stops on a dime. I see the edges of its head behind a tree and yell loudly to try and intimidate it. What I heard next I'll never forget in my entire life. It cackled like a monkey. A noise I've literally only heard in nature documentaries. The tone was that of mockery; a predator having fun with me. I didn't stick around. I sprinted as fast as possible back home.

I'd love to believe this was some prank or some rabid, bald, diseased coyote but I got a pretty clear look at it. It wasn't. It had human feet and human hands. A human head and human buttocks. But nothing else about it was human. I called the cops after and told them a man was following me. I didn't want to say some creature because they'd think I'm crazy. They didn't find anything but they did see quite a bit of activity in the leaves and dirt about 50 feet from where the trail was, leading far back into the woods before it got to a large stretch of grass where no footprints were seen."

34

SAM

NAME OF EYEWITNESS	Sam
DATE/TIME OF SIGHTING	August 27th, 2020 after 7 a.m.
LOCATION OF SIGHTING	Berlin, New Hampshire.
CIRCUMSTANCES PRIOR TO SIGHTING	On an early morning walk.
NOTABLE SIGHTING DETAILS	Ape-like facial features.

Initial statement

"I live in western New Hampshire and I think I saw something on a walk. I know I am not close to the four corners and I know that may make this hard to believe but I know that I saw something.

I woke up at 7 a.m. to walk to a park to see my buddies which was my first mistake: walking alone. Usually, I carry a knife on me when I go anywhere alone but that morning I did not. I started walking down my street and had a strong feeling of dread and fatigue. I turned onto a gravel road and saw a figure light gray and about 5'5. Its arms were down to its knees and it was just there slouched over.

I stared at it for around 15 seconds then built up the courage to start running. Once I got in my house my dog started growling. He is a golden retriever, so that's very rare. I locked the door and ran up to my room with my dog at my side. I peeked out of the window and saw it peeking just behind the tree line. I pulled out my phone but it had already run away."

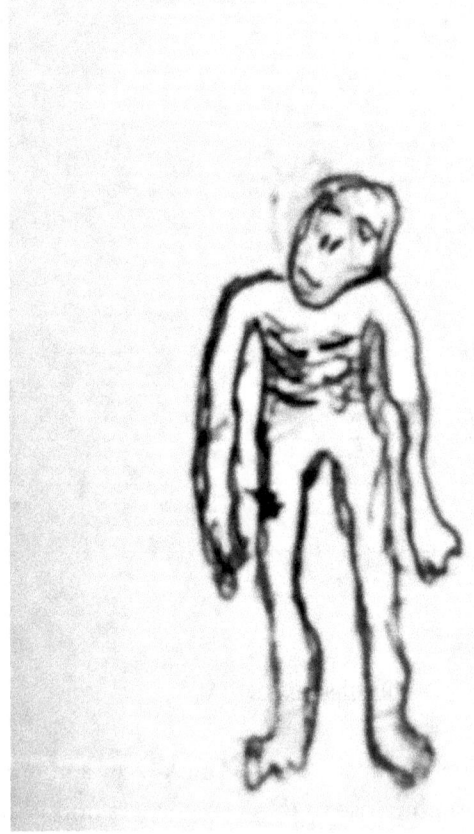

Eyewitness sketch provided by Sam.

35

ANONYMOUS 10

NAME OF EYEWITNESS	Anonymous.
DATE/TIME OF SIGHTING	January 3rd, 2021.
LOCATION OF SIGHTING	Housenick Park, Bethlehem, PA.
CIRCUMSTANCES PRIOR TO SIGHTING	Extreme emotional trauma.
NOTABLE SIGHTING DETAILS	Orange-skinned subject with a long nose.

Initial statement

"I need help. January of this year was a very dark place for me emotionally. My husband and I grew estranged after the loss of our six-day-old youngest son. For about two months, December and January, we were apart as he spiraled into substance abuse to numb the pain. He left town and stayed with his father across the state. When he came back into town we wanted to see each other.

He checked into a hotel in Bethlehem, Pennsylvania. I drove out to see him around 7:00 p.m. when our then two-year-old son fell asleep. We were staying with my mother during this time and she offered to watch our little one. I stayed for a few hours. It was very emotional, to say the least. We wanted to reconcile and overcome the tragedy we had faced. Around 12:00 p.m.-ish I knew I would have to get back to my mother's house in case our son woke up. It was pitch black outside and my GPS led me down a narrow road. I was eager to get home and although very overwhelmed, wide awake due to the adrenaline of seeing my husband for the first time after our 'separation.' I crossed over a stream and started going slightly uphill. In the middle of the road was a set of bright green eyes. I instantly slowed down because there are a ton of deer in the area. If there is one deer there is usually more. I slowly crept up the hill in my minivan, scanning for more eyes, and the figure in the middle of the road scuttled to the right-hand side and then stayed perfectly still and positioned. 'Scuttled' is the only way to describe the way it moved honestly.

To the right was a big open field and some trees and brush that lined the perimeter alongside the road. The thing was along the brush almost like it was trying to blend in. It was on both its hands and feet; its arms were unnaturally long and bent at an angle. Its eyes were that reflective green the entire time I drove past it with no pupils. I don't think it looked at me directly, after it positioned itself in the brush it stared past me with a black hole for a mouth; not gaping but wide open.

Since I slowed down quite a bit to prevent myself hitting what I thought was a deer, I got a good long look at it. About 8-ish feet tall but on all fours, crouched. Skin looked like orange bark like it was trying to camouflage along the trees but it was too orange/tan and as I crept closer I saw that it was fleshy like gross, orangey-swollen bloody flesh.

The nose is what stood out to me [the most]. It was long and pointy, I'd almost compare it to Pinocchio before he would tell a lie. All the same orangey fleshy color. I hope that makes sense, I don't really know how else to describe it. It happened in seconds. I thought I saw a deer, I slowed down as I passed it and it was NOT a f–king deer. I kept driving. Almost immediately after I laid my eyes on it I felt my heartbeat in my throat. Such a horrific sense of dread consumed me and it almost helped me continue to act rationally and drive the hell away from there. I then heard a knocking and a huge thud come from the inside of my van like someone had jumped from the back but on the inside. All of my windows were up because it was obviously winter so there was no logical way something could have suddenly appeared as I was driving. All of the hair stood up on the back of my neck and every instinct I had was telling me to keep staring straight ahead. Do NOT look behind, do NOT look in the rearview mirror, do NOT say a f–king word, so I didn't.

I struggled to breathe. I had a huge lump in my throat as I sped down that road, so beyond scared with every fiber of my being on overdrive telling me to GET AWAY FROM THERE. The second I turned off of that road, that feeling of someone being in the car with me was gone. I looked back and nobody was there. I kept driving and called my husband in hysterics, half sobbing, half laughing out of shock and saying, "I'm not scared, I'd kick its ass," because I had a feeling it thrived off of my fear. It was one of the most terrifying things I have ever experienced in my life.

Months have passed since then. My husband and I have since reconciled and have been even stronger since our fallout. We have tried to look more into it but every time we started to do more research I would get a sick feeling in my stomach, almost like my body was warning me to leave it be. I tried to ignore it and forget it for the longest time.

My husband and I bought a piece of property locally. As we looked at properties we stayed away from anything big and open with a field because it reminded me too much of that thing. We purchased a heavily wooded lot about 30 miles away from where this experience took place. We are having a home built custom to our three-year-old son's needs (our little guy has cerebral palsy). We move onto the property next week in a camper to oversee construction but now I'm worried. What if there is another encounter and I have my little boy with me this time? What if something bad happens and I lose him? I already lost one son... if anything happened to my oldest I don't know what I'd do.

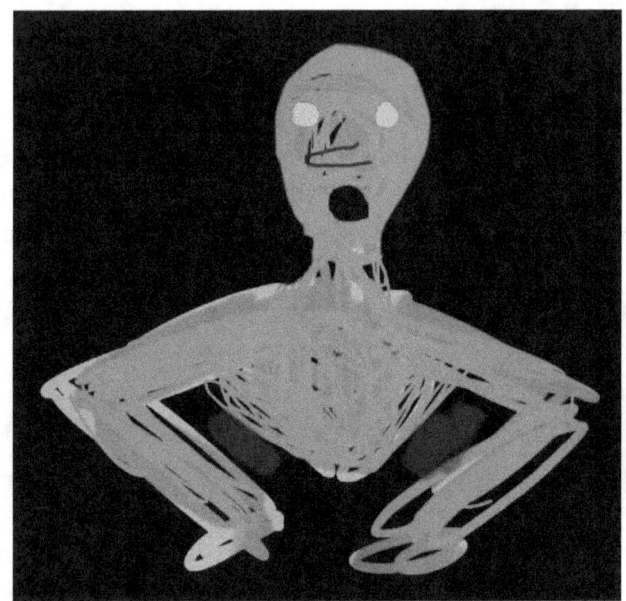

Original artistic depiction by the eyewitness.

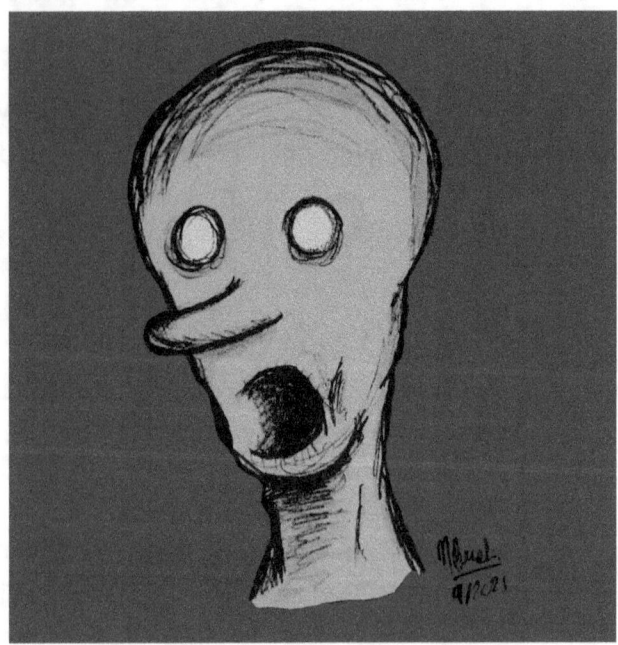

Bottom refined depiction created by the author.

We began finally really digging into what that thing was. We looked into the thing itself based off of its appearance and the location I saw it at. It turns out that the field I saw it at was a part of a memorial park called Housenick Park. There was a lot of Native American history tied into that area so we dug more into local lore. We came across the term "skinwalker." That was probably the closest thing we found that resembled the creature. That's what we've been referring to it as but there were a few things about my encounter and its appearances that still make me hesitant to believe with 100% certainty that is what it was. I have a sketch I drew that might be of some help but I'm no artist."

Illustrated head study by the author with input from the eyewitness. The eyewitness was quoted as saying, "Scary accurate. In my sketch, I drew the eyes a little too far apart from what they were in real life. Seriously, the sketch is so accurate that it gave me goosebumps and sent a shiver down my spine. Thank you so much for taking the time to draw that. I've tried a few times and I couldn't draw it right which left me so frustrated."

A SCIENTIST'S VIEW ON CRAWLERS
BY "POLOMARCEL"

I am a zoologist working in a natural history museum and my job is literally to describe new species. I wanted to give some of my thoughts on Crawlers from a scientific point of view.

What first struck me is the consistency of all the descriptions of the animal throughout the reported sightings which contributes to making it credible in my opinion as well as the restricted geographical distribution of the sightings, i.e. they are not seen all over the world but mostly in North America which is consistent with a real animal having a natural distribution area.

Some found a correlation between the presence of caves and Crawler sightings. I find this particularly interesting since Crawlers seem to present most of the characters that evolved in cave species, namely loss of skin pigmentation, elongation of the limbs reduction/loss of the eyes, slow metabolism due to the lack of food (which agrees with the reported emaciated body), and nocturnal foraging behavior.

From the descriptions, it seems that Crawlers are bipedal humanoids so we can assume that this animal would probably be a primate. Except for humans, there are no apes (Catarrhini) in America as they evolved separately in the Old World, so Crawlers would be members of the Platyrrhini, a group comprising all the currently extant American monkeys. Monkeys are now absent from North America but they used to live there until the end of the Eocene epoch about 33 million years ago when climate changes led them to disappear from there and become restricted to tropical areas. Maybe some individuals found refuge or were trapped in cave systems around this time and evolved to become the Crawlers. Caves are indeed known to serve as refuges for animal groups that disappeared from the surface.

To date, the only vertebrates to have been found living in caves are some fish and a few amphibians. If the existence of a cave-dwelling primate in North America was proven to be true, it would be a huge breakthrough, 1: as the first known cave mammal ever; 2: as the only known primate in North America.

Now imagine a hairless and tailless spider monkey. Wouldn't it make a convincing Crawler?

— **Anonymous zoologist**

THE FUTURE OF CRAWLER
CRYPTOZOOLOGY

A photograph allegedly captured in 2008 at King's Cliff near North Petherton, Somerset, England implying the existence of possible Crawler encounters outside of North America. (Enhanced for clarity)

Cryptozoology, defined by the brain, is the study of unknown animals. Defined by the heart, though, it is a community that knows no bounds in terms of support for others in their quest to find the truth. From that support, so many incredibly important things are born; things like art, shared research, the ability to connect with another who has shared a similar experience to you, and from there, detailed accounts of sightings of weird and unique creatures from across North America.

This book is the product of one man's hard work, determination and open-mindedness as well as a community's willingness to share what they've experienced. The future of Pale Crawler research will require the same.

Nathaniel Brislin has been collecting these encounters for years to bring a cohesive and detailed resource together for those who wish to find the truth about the Pale Crawlers. This research is the biggest collection of information on these terrifying creatures to date and for that, we thank him and his community. Going forward, the future of Pale Crawler research will prove to be an effort by the community as a whole, with this book laying the groundwork and foundation for this investigation.

Kenzie Gleason (@cryptidbaddie)

Host of **Cryptozoology Chats Podcast**
& Manic Pixie Dream Ghouls

AFTERWORD

Go to hangarıpublishing.com to learn more about the Author and stay up to date with their newest releases.

JAKY & NICK C. AND OTHERS

Born and raised in the state of Maine, Nathaniel Brislin has always had an interest in life on Earth both living and extinct; known and unknown. Nate is an artist, writer, and filmmaker who has released two documentaries; **Pine State Phantoms** (2019) and **Eyes from the Pines: The Pine Ape Project** (2021).

www.ingramcontent.com/pod-product-compliance
Lightning Source LLC
Chambersburg PA
CBHW071147120626
46546CB00006B/2158

* 9 7 8 1 9 5 5 4 7 1 7 0 1 *